Wooden Chess Sets You Can Make

By Diana Thompson

FOX CHAPEL
PUBLISHING

Acknowledgments

Thank you Father for the over abundance of blessing. I'm grateful You find me worthy.
Thanks Captain for the chess board help. I couldn't have done it without you!
Thank you Ayleen for your encouragement, guidance and your faith that I could do the job!

© 2003 by Fox Chapel Publishing Company, Inc.

Wooden Chess Sets You Can Make is an original work, first published in 2003 by Fox Chapel Publishing Compa Inc. The patterns contained herein are copyrighted by the author. Artists may make photocopies of the each individual pattern for personal use only. The patterns themselves, however, are not to be duplicated for resale distribution under any circumstances. This is a violation of copyright law.

Publisher	Alan Giagnocavo
Project Editor	Ayleen Stellhorn
Desktop Specialist	Alan Davis
Cover Design	Tim Mize
Interior Gallery Photos	Harry Troutman

ISBN 978-1-56523-188-7
Library of Congress Preassigned Card Number:
2002117851

To learn more about the other great books from Fox Chapel Publishing,
or to find a retailer near you, call toll-free 1-800-457-9112 or
visit us at **www.FoxChapelPublishing.com**.

Note to Authors: we are always looking for talented authors to write new books in our area of woodworking, design, and related crafts. Please send a brief letter describing your idea to Acquisition Editor, 1970 Broad Street, East Petersburg, PA 17520.

Printed in China
First printing
Second printing
Third printing

Table of Contents

About the Author

Diana Thompson enjoys designing creative patterns for compound scrolling almost as much as she enjoys her time sinking putts on the golf courses near her home in Alabama. She has authored three other books of her patterns and techniques: 3D Patterns for the Scroll Saw, Scroll Saw Compound Creations, and Compound Christmas Ornaments. You can visit Diana online at *www.scrollsawinspirations.com* or e-mail her at info@scrollsawinspirations.com.

Welcome to the world of compound sawing: The simple technique of making two cuts on one pattern to create a three-dimensional piece. Be prepared to embark on a new journey, one that is guaranteed to keep you enthralled and forever in your workshop.

These new patterns were done at the request of my editor, Ayleen Stellhorn. My first inclination was to say no because I didn't have a clue as to where to begin. As time went along, and with suggestions from Ayleen and others, this book began to develop—and I'm so glad I didn't refuse to do it.

At this point, I must admit, I'm not a chess player. Ayleen has offered to teach me, but there's a good chance I'll be a lost cause. However, after doing some research I find the history of the game most fascinating.

A Brief History of the Game of Chess

While researching this subject, I've come to the conclusion no one knows the exact origin of chess. The most popularly held theory seems to be that the game of chess began in India around A.D. 600. From there it spread to Asia, China and Persia, and then reached Europe at A.D. 1100.

The original pieces on the chess board were based on military strategy and included infantry, cavalry, elephants and chariots of the ancient Indian army. At that time there was no queen in the game, but rather a vizier who represented the spiritual advisor to the king. As the game become more popular in Europe, the figures were changed to represent the medieval times of Europe. The king remained as such, and the pawns remained as infantry or foot soldiers. The queen replaced the vizier, and the elephant was replaced by the bishop, who was considered the spiritual adviser to the king and represented the church or religion during these times.

By the end of the 15th century, the rules of chess began to change and the queen became the most powerful piece on the board. It's thought that the queens of medieval times held much power and sway over their king, even though this power was often wielded with intrigue and secrecy to maintain her position of power. A queen who chose not to do so could be set aside as easily as a snap of the fingers at that time. But although the queen is the most powerful piece on the board, she is not the most important. If the king is captured, the game is over.

The knight represents the cavalry of medieval times. His job was to protect persons of note. In this case, the chessboard knight protects the king, the queen and the bishop.

The castle, or rook as it is sometimes called, represents the shelter or place of refuge as it was in medieval times. The castle guards the outer edges of the chess board.

Over time, the pawns on the chess board were thought of not so much as foot soldiers but as surfs or peons. They are the most lowly of pieces on the chess board and can be sacrificed to save the other, more important figures. Each side has one king, one queen, two bishops, two knights, two rooks and eight pawns.

My hope is that you will find scrolling chess sets as much fun as I did.

Enjoy,
Diana Thompson
info@scrollsawinspirations.com

Part One

Compound Basics

Compound, or 3D sawing as it is sometimes called, is simply making two cuts on the same working stock. For such a simple idea, this method of scrolling turns out fascinating results.

Safety First

First and foremost, keep safety in mind at all times when you are using power tools. Make sure all your equipment is working properly before you begin. Wearing a dust mask is important, as some woods are irritants and sensitizers that can cause health problems. Do not wear loose clothing around

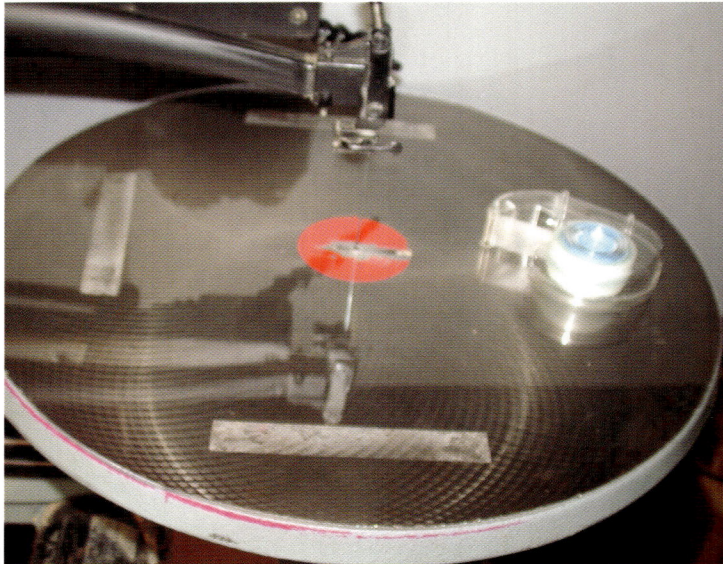

Saw tables are sometimes uneven. A homemade Plexiglas™ cover for your saw table will ensure that you are cutting on a perfectly even surface.

machinery because it can catch in moving parts and cause bodily injury. Always wear safety glasses to protect your eyes. Also, remember to use common sense and to give yourself frequent breaks.

Helpful Tips
The saw table

For compound sawing, it's very important to have a perfectly flat surface. Sometimes the table insert is not always flush with the table. This causes the work to fall down into an uneven area and will result in a

Use a carpenter's square with a level to check that your blade is running at a perfect 90° angle to your saw table. A square block of wood can also be used to check the blade's alignment.

figure that comes out uneven. To solve this problem, cut a piece of Plexiglas™ the size of your table and drill a small ¼" hole in the center. A few pieces of two-sided tape will hold the Plexiglas™ securely to the table. Polish the Plexiglas™ surface every now and then with an ordinary paste wax to keep it smooth.

The blades

All the patterns are cut with a #5 single or skip tooth blade. I don't recommend a reverse tooth blade as it tends to slow the work down when cutting the 1½" stock.

Make sure your blade is moving at a perfect 90° angle to your saw table before you start to cut. I

Making a 1¹/₂" block

Stock that is 1½" deep is difficult to find. You can create your own blocks by purchasing readily available ¾" wood and gluing two pieces together as shown below.

Step 1:
Sand the ¾" stock and apply wood glue to one side.

Step 2:
Sandwich the two pieces of stock together and use small Quick Grips on each end to hold the two pieces securely in place.

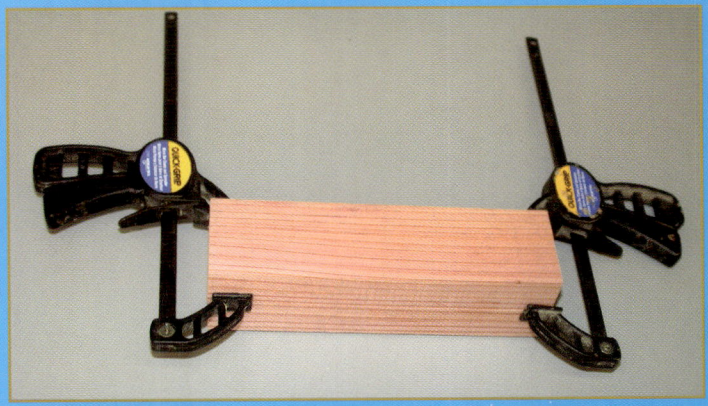

Step 3:
Apply pony clamps, remove the Quick Grips, and allow the glue to set up for at least half an hour.

Double check the blade's alignment with this simple method. Make a cut and back the blade out of the cut. Then move the wood to the back of the saw blade and try to back the running blade into the kerf. If the blade moves in easily, your blade is correctly aligned.

recommend checking the blade alignment each time you use your saw. Use a small square to do a quick check.

Just leveling the saw table will not guarantee that the blade is properly aligned. Designer legend John Nelson teaches the easiest way of checking the proper alignment: Make a small ½" cut into a 1" piece of wood. Turn the wood to the back of the blade and try backing the moving blade into the kerf. If the blade doesn't go in easily, consult your owner's manual for instructions on how to realign the blade.

Tension the blade properly. Before you begin, pluck the blade and listen for a nice, clear "ping." A dull "thud" means the tension is too loose. Tighten the tension a little at a time until the sound is clear. If the blade tends to squirm around like a worm, making it hard to follow the lines while cutting, chances are the blade is too loose. Your owner's manual will give you the details on how to change the tension for your particular saw.

Change the blade often. The #5 blade runs at 1800 strokes per minute without breaking. As the blade dulls, you will find yourself exerting more pressure to cut the thick wood, and more pressure often results in misshapen figures.

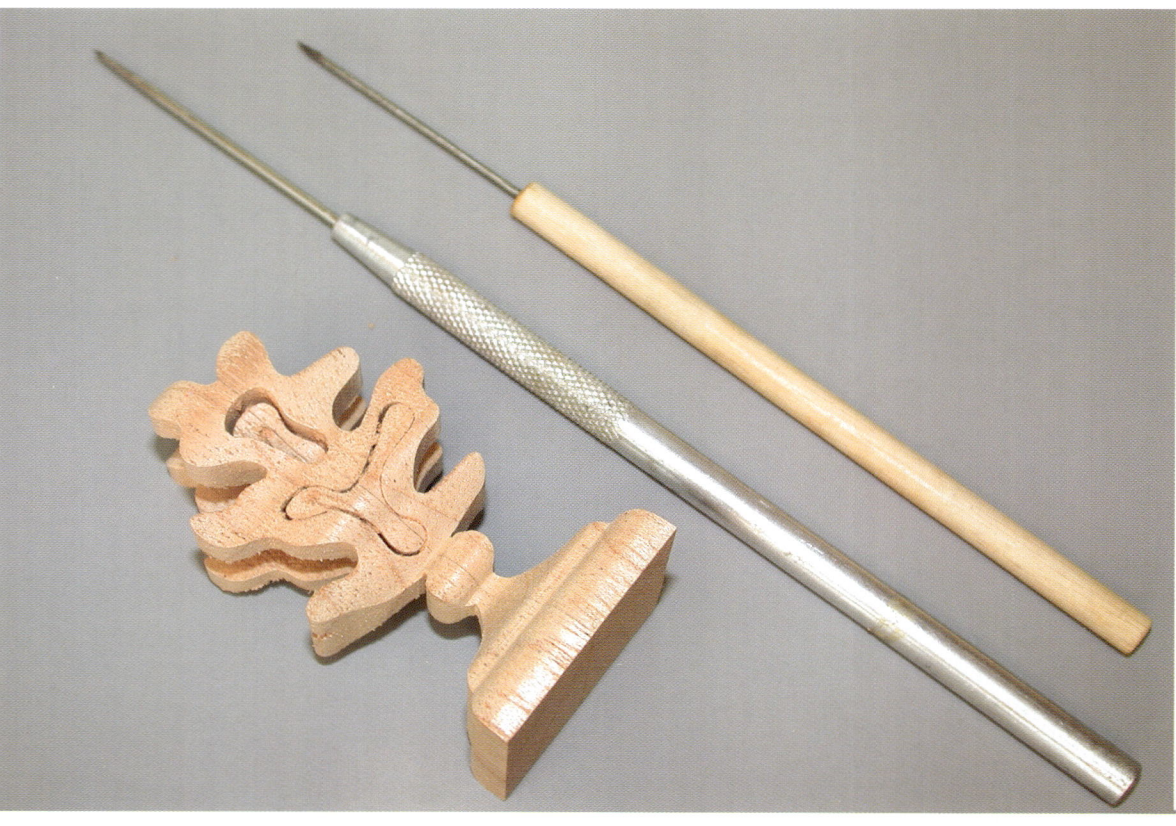

A stiletto is an ideal tool for removing small pieces of wood from the inside cuts.

When cutting the second side of the pattern, be sure not to push the block from the bottom. This will cause the figure to shift out of place on the inside and result in an uneven finished figure.

The wood

All the patterns in this book call for 1½" stock, which is pretty thick for the scroll saw, especially if you are working in harder woods. Try applying clear packing tape over the wood to make the blade cut faster and easier. The tape is quite shiny and will cause a glare under the shop lights, so be sure to apply the pattern over the tape.

The choice of what wood to use is limitless. You can choose a wood as soft as sugar or white pine or as dense as red oak. Some good hardwood choices for compound scrolling are black walnut, canary, willow, western and red cedar. Sugar pine, white pine or basswood are good choices if you plan to paint your finished piece with craft paints.

It isn't always easy to find 1½" stock needed for the patterns in this book; however, ¾" stock is quite common and is usually more economically priced. Simply glue two pieces of ¾" stock together with wood glue and secure them with pony clamps. The clamps are very inexpensive and found at most home improvement stores. When the glue dries, you'll have a block of 1½" stock. The wood for each figure in this book was glued-up with the method on page 3.

Trouble Shooting

If your figures are coming off the saw uneven or misshapen, check the following list for potential reasons for the unwanted result.

- The blade could be too loose. Tighten the tension.
- You may be pushing too hard on the block. This will cause the blade to over-flex, resulting in lopsided figures. Use lighter pressure as you feed the wood through the saw.
- You may be pushing the blade sideways. Make sure you're feeding the line directly into the blade. Turn the work into the blade, and not sideways trying to get back on track.
- The surface of your saw table may be uneven. Cut a Plexiglas™ cover to fit your table as shown on page 2.
- You may be pushing the block from the bottom on the second cut. This will tend to move the inside figure out of alignment.

Making Interior Cuts

When using a pattern that has inside cuts, also known as frets, be sure to make the inside cuts first.

Step 1. Drill a small hole with a 1/16" drill bit.

Step 2. Thread the blade through the drill hole and cut the fret.

Step 3. Leave the fret in place.

Step 4. Turn the block and make the interior cuts on the second side.

Step 5. Leave the fret in place.

Step 6. Now move on to cut the outside lines of the figure.

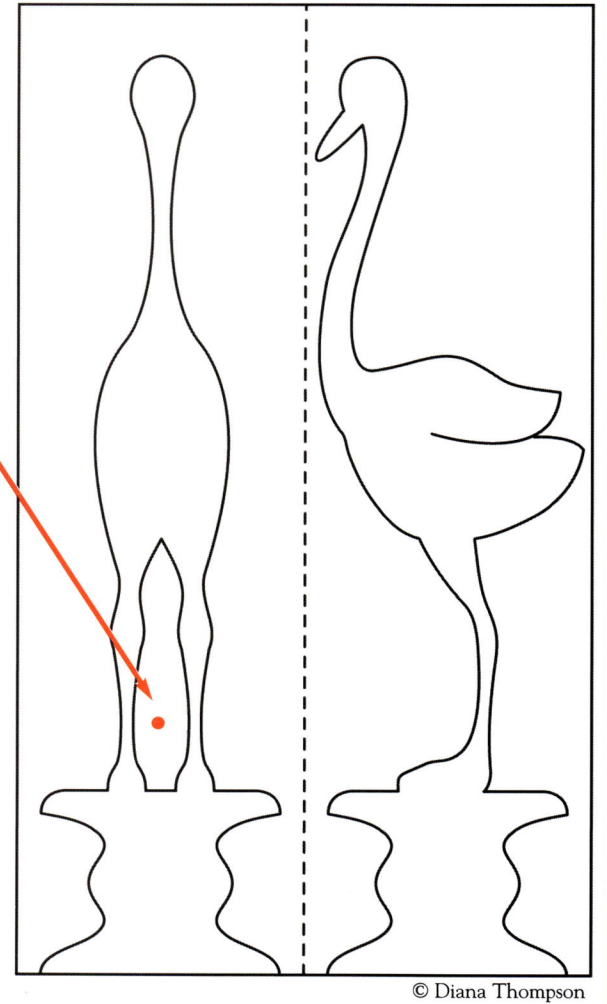

© Diana Thompson

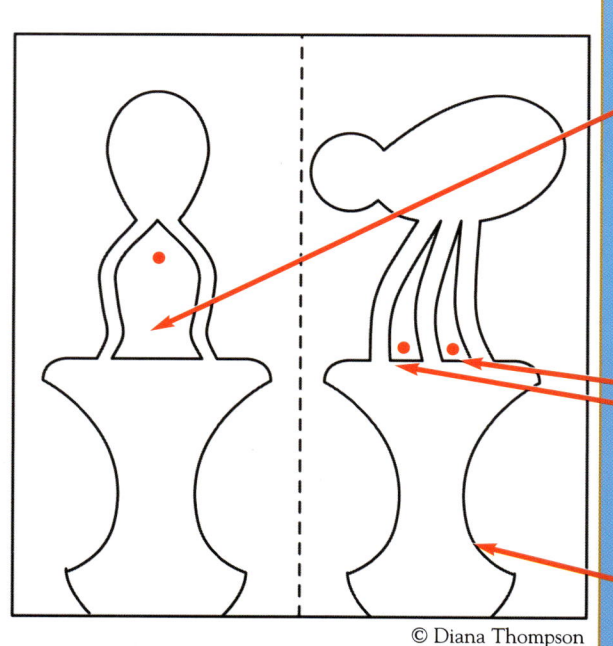

© Diana Thompson

Cut this fret first

Cut these frets next

Cut the outlines last

Finishing

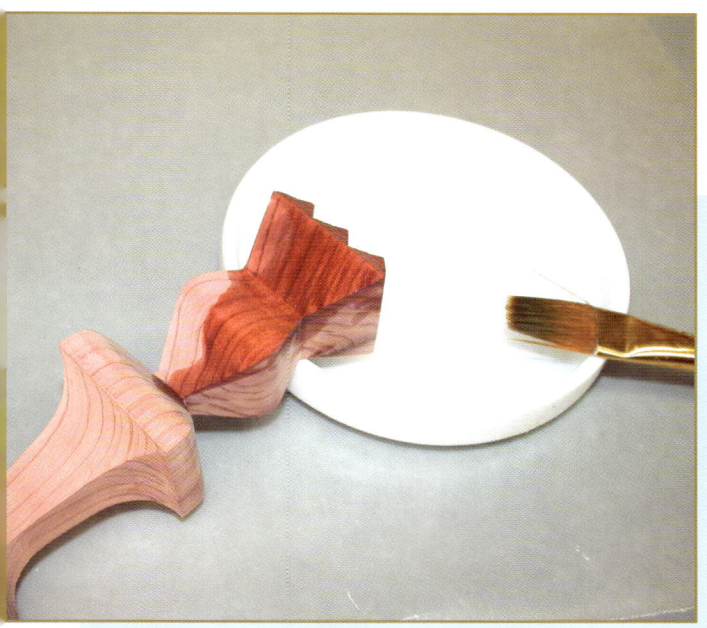

...utcher block or salad bowl finish is an excellent choice for pieces that will be handled a lot. The finish is non-...xic and cleans up easily with soap and water. Use a paint brush to apply butcher block or salad bowl finish ... the cut pieces (left). Allow the piece to absorb the finish for five minutes, then wipe off the excess (right).

For a nice natural finish, seal the pieces with wood sealer, then sand them smooth with 220 grit sandpaper. Finish with several coats of clear satin polycrylic.

Different colors of acrylic craft paint can also be used to differentiate between opposing sides. Seal the pieces with wood sealer, sand them smooth with 220-grit sandpaper, then paint them with acrylic craft paints of your choice.

Crackle

Step 1. Apply several medium thick coats of acrylic craft paint. Choose your favorite brand. Allow it to dry at least four hours.

Step 2. Apply a single coat of the crackle mediu[m]. The thicker the medium is applied, the bigger [the] crackles. This is a medium-thick application. T[he] cracks will begin to appear as the medium dries.

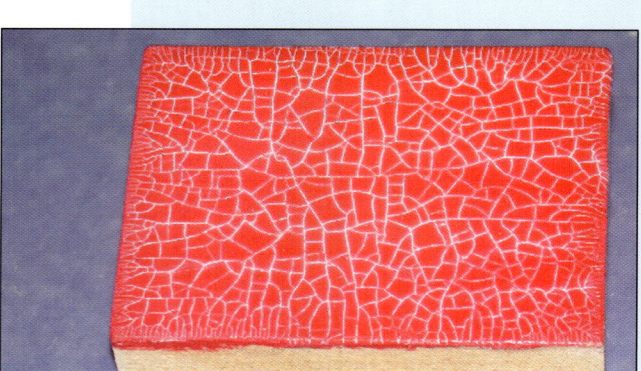

Step 3. After the project dried, I used white acrylic paint to fill in the cracks. Rub it on with your fingers, and wipe excess off with a dry cloth. You may want to thin the paint just a little, but don't over-do it.

This is a sample [of] how the finish[ed] projects can loo[k.] It's a very easy f[in-] ishing techniq[ue] but looks impre[s-] sive. Apply a cl[ear] spray finish to p[ro-] tect the surface, a[nd] you're done. (No[te:] Patterns not inclu[d-] ed in this book.)

Flocking

Flocking gives a smooth, felt-like texture to your projects. Apply the glue in a smooth, generous coat. Immediately apply the fibers. Don't shake or tap the fibers off. Allow your project to dry at least an hour before handling it. Brush off the excess fibers and return them to the bottle.

When using flocking on [a] compound figure, fi[rst] apply a water-base sea[ler] to your project. Allow it [to] dry, then sand it smo[oth] with 220-grit sandpap[er.] Follow the applicati[on] directions on the bott[le.] The details are eas[ily] applied over the dry floc[k-] ing with acrylic cr[aft] paints and a small brus[h.] (Note: Pattern not inclu[ded] in this book.)

Sandstone

This is a simple finish called Sandstone by DecoArt. It has a stone-like quality. Simply apply the color of choice, allow it to dry, then apply the next color. It can be top coated with a clear acrylic spray, but it isn't necessary. I prefer leaving it natural, as the texture has a quite pleasing effect.

Apply a water base sealer to your project. Allow it to dry, then sand smooth with 220 or higher grit sandpaper. Apply colors one at a time, using a relatively heavy coat for perfect coverage. Allow it to dry before adding additional colors. (Note: Pattern not included in this book.)

The finished project.

Goldleaf

For this finishing technique, I've used a gold leafing kit, found at most craft stores. It's a very easy and quick process.

The first step is to apply a sealer to your project, allow it to dry, and sand it smooth with 220 grit sandpaper. Then add a base coat of color, if desired.

Apply one coat of the adhesive. It will be cloudy when first applied. Allow it to dry until it becomes clear.

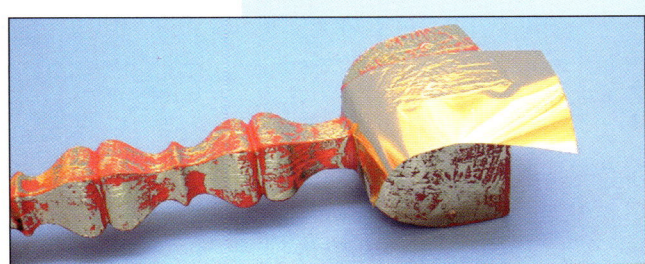

Apply the gold leafing, matte side down, rubbing it firmly with your fingers. Pull the sheet away. The leafing will adhere to your project. Continue this process until your project is covered. A clear coat finish can be applied, if desired, upon completion.

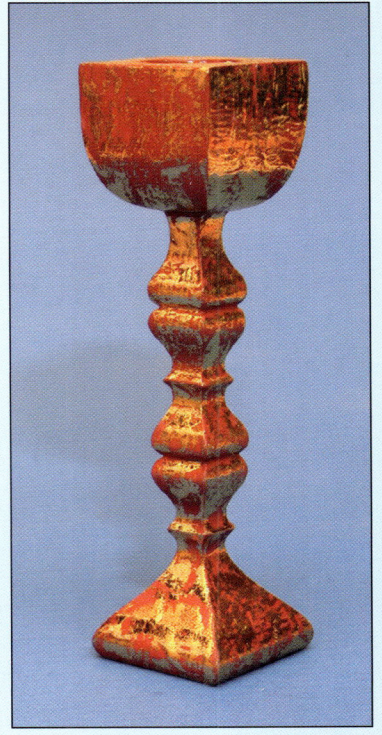

I chose to allow the red craft paint of the base coat to show through the gold. The base coat can be covered completely with additional applications of the gold leaf. (Note: Pattern not included in this book.)

Part Two

General Directions

Now the fun begins! Follow these general directions to cut all of the pieces in this book. Remember to cut to the waste side of the lines for the best results. Cutting directly on the line can result in too much material being removed. This can cause the more delicate areas of the patterns to break.

Cutting a Chess Piece

Cut the pattern out along the heavy rectangular line. Do not cut the two pieces apart on the dotted line. Apply spray adhesive to the back of the pattern. Place the pattern on the block, wrapping the pattern around two sides of the block.

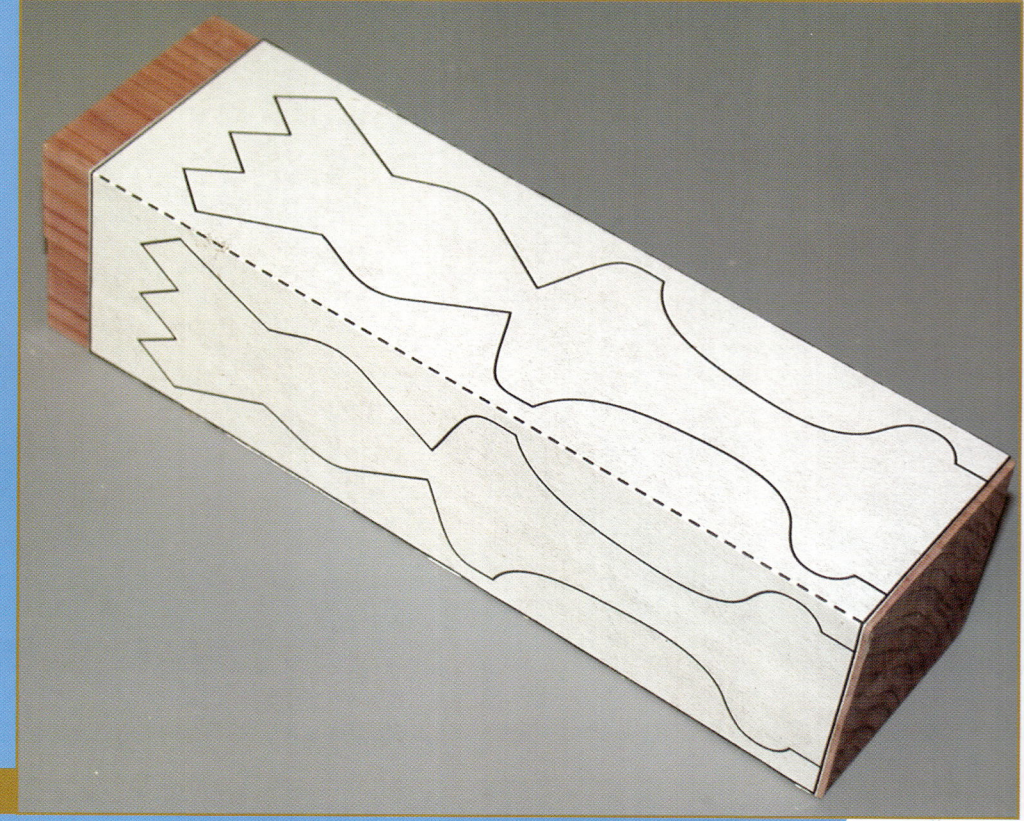

1

Sand or cut the bottom of the piece to the pattern line so that the figure will stand level when it's finished.

2

Cut the left side in one continuous line. Remember to cut to the waste side of the lines to avoid removing too much material, which can result in a weak or broken figure. Note: The spare blocks attached to the figure give me a little more area to hold onto. Tighten the grips only enough to hold the work steady; not so tight that the blade cannot move freely through the wood.

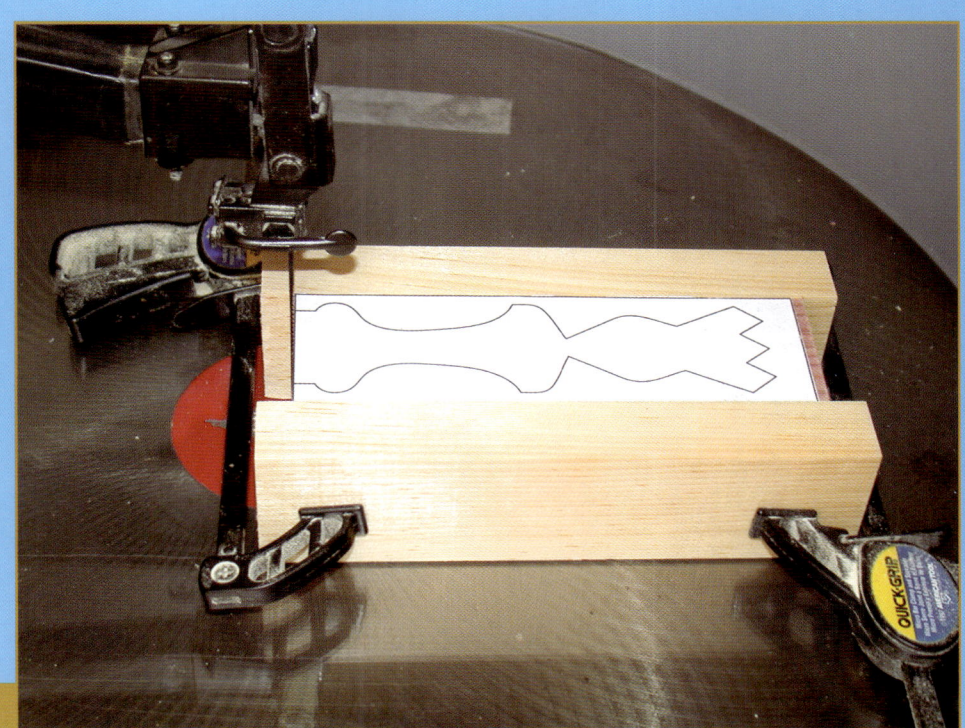

3

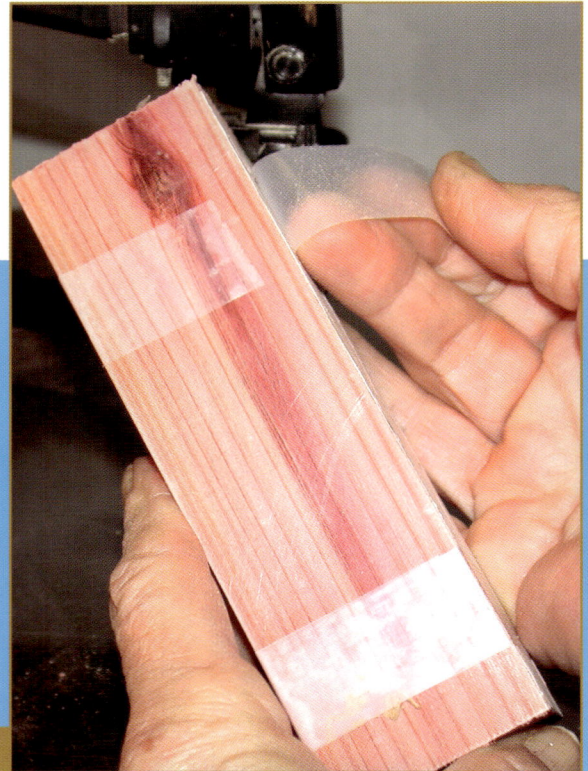

5 Tap the block on the saw table a few times to ensure the figure is seated properly inside.

4 Allowing the figure to rest naturally in the block, pinch it together slightly and tape around the block in two places with 3/4" cellophane tape.

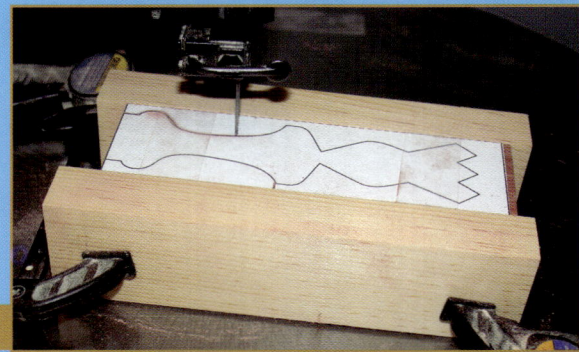

6 Cut the right side of the pattern in one continuous line.

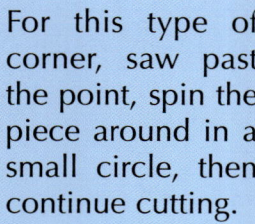

7 Gently remove the figure from the block.

Turning Corners

Corners can be tricky areas to cut for beginning and advanced scrollers alike. Use these tips to make your corners crisp.

At this type of corner, pause and make sure that the blade is moving perfectly straight up and down with no stress from any direction on it. Then turn the corner quickly

For this type of corner, saw past the point, spin the piece around in a small circle, then continue cutting.

Chess Set Patterns

On the following pages you will find patterns for nine complete chess sets. These sets range from traditional to whimsical to out-of-this-world. Each piece should be cut following the general directions in Part Two of this book. All are cut from 1½" stock. If you intend to leave the pieces with a natural finish, choose a type of wood from the "Wood Appendix" at the end of this book. Note that some woods are harder than others and will take more skill and patience to cut.

Once you are comfortable cutting chess sets, try your hand at designing your own patterns or altering the patterns featured here.

Classic One   **14**

Classic Two   **19**

For the Birds   **24**

Happy Bugs   **29**

In the Garden   **34**

Sea Life   **39**

Alien Chess   **44**

Woodworker's Set   **49**

Honorable Heritage   **54**

Classic I

This chess set is modeled after a traditional chess set based on medieval times. The king and queen are easily recognized by the different style of their head pieces: The king's is pointed; the queen's is rounded. The remaining pieces follow suit. The bishop represents an actual bishop from this time period; the knight is a knight's horse; the rook is a castle turret; and the pawn is a surf.

Cut each set from a different kind of wood to make each distinctive. This set is cut from black walnut.

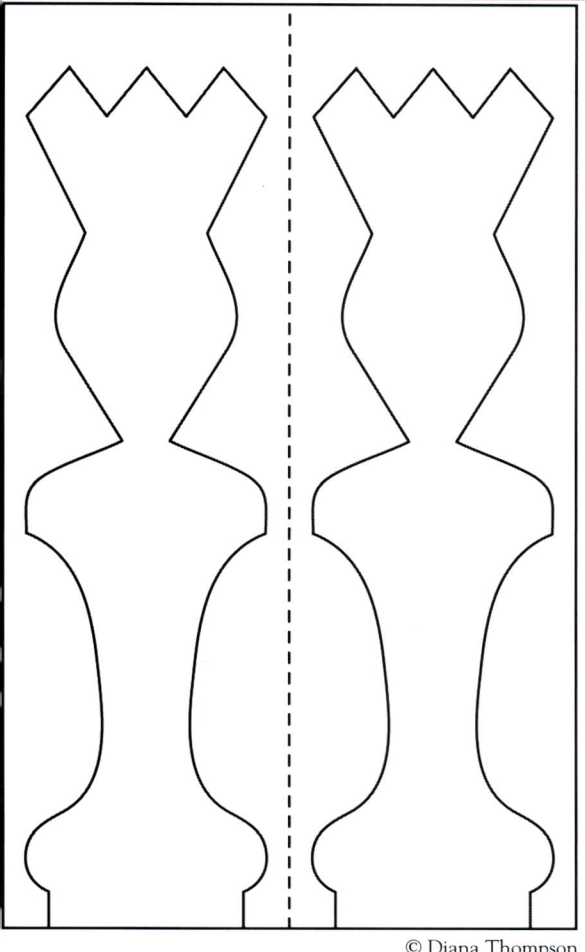

© Diana Thompson

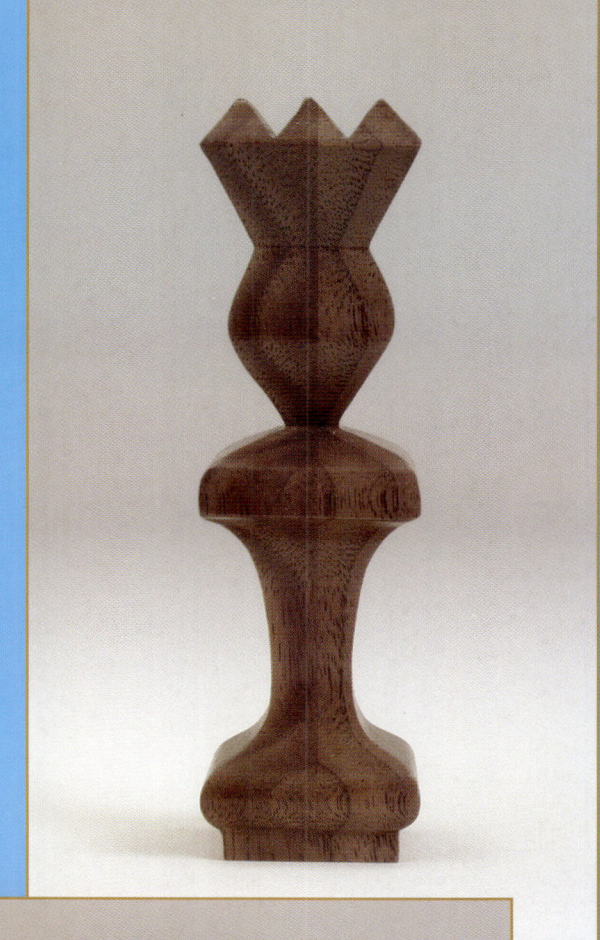

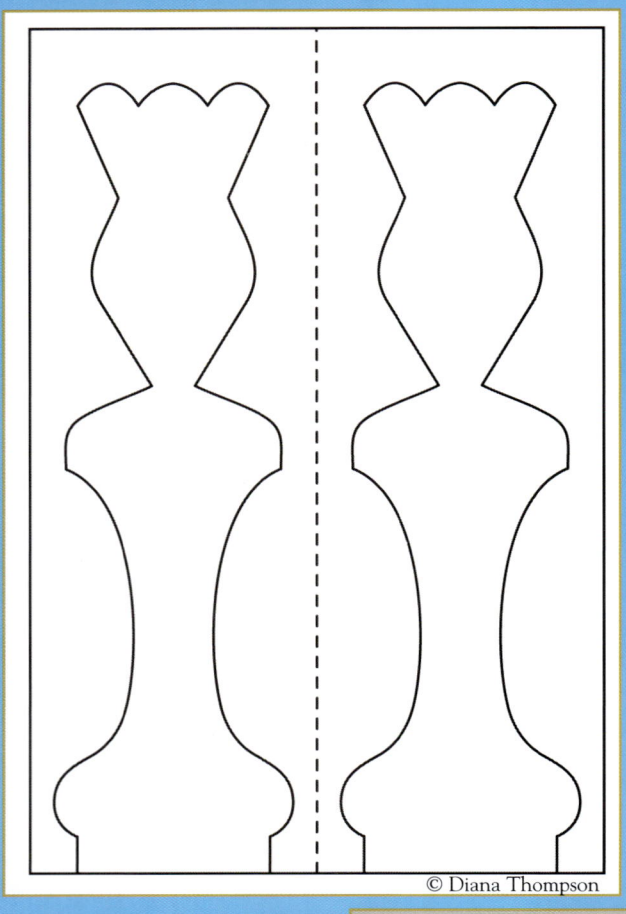

© Diana Thompson

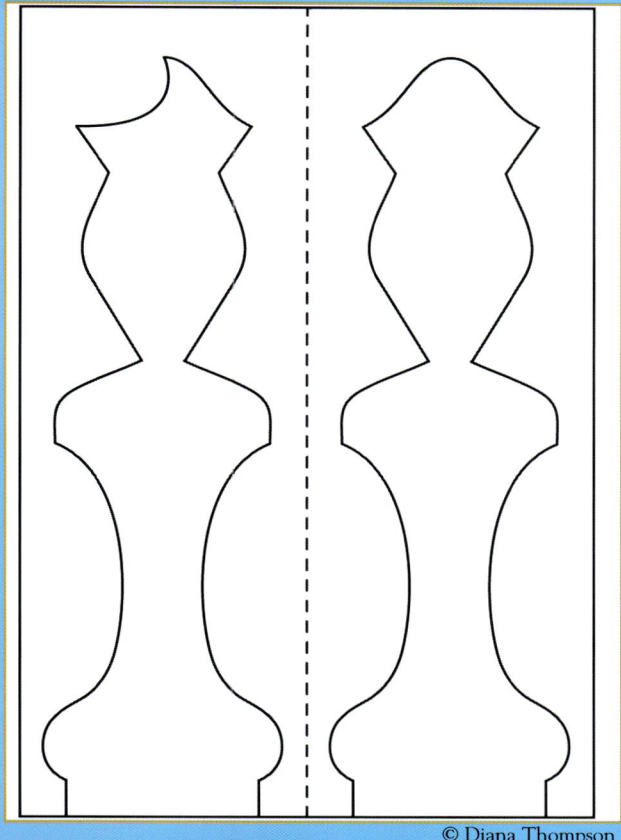

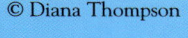

© Diana Thompson

assic I: Knight

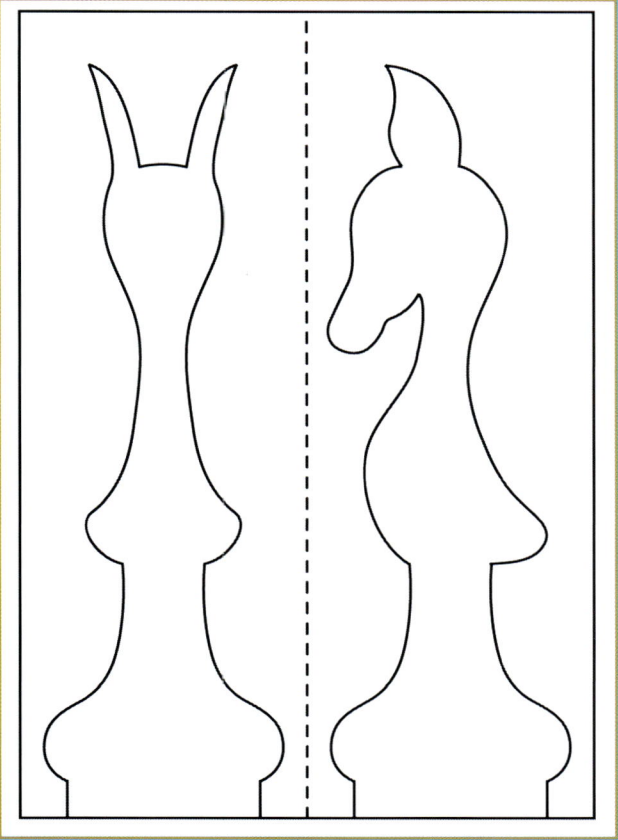

© Diana Thompson

Classic I: Rook

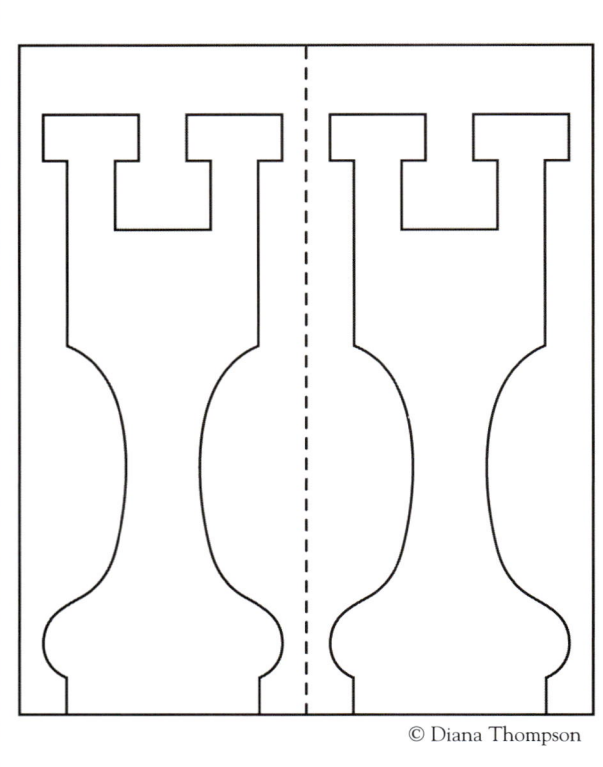

© Diana Thompson

Classic I: Pawn

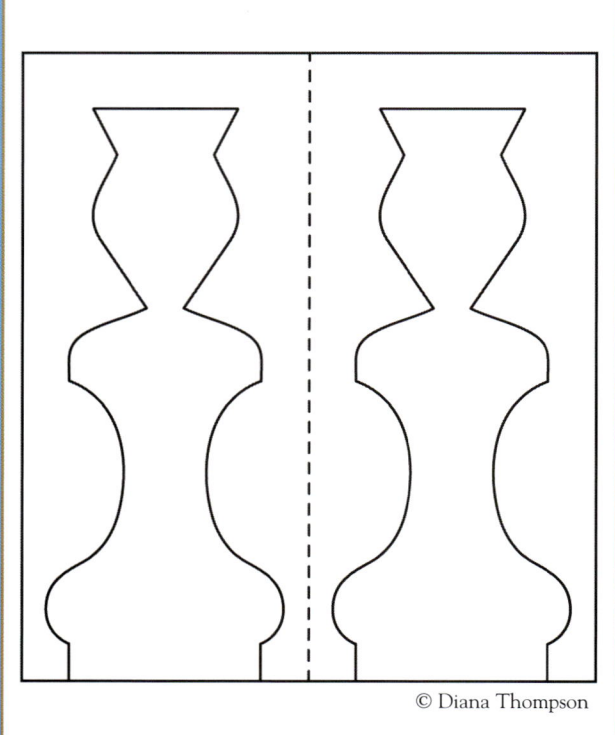

© Diana Thompson

Classic II

Another traditional chess set, this group does not include any characters that look like people. The king is recognized by the pointed spade at the top of the piece; the queen's is round. The bishop is topped with a cross, and the knight is a horse. The rook represents a castle turret. The pawn is the smallest piece with a sharp point at the top.

Cut each set from a different kind of wood to make each distinctive. This set is cut from canary wood.

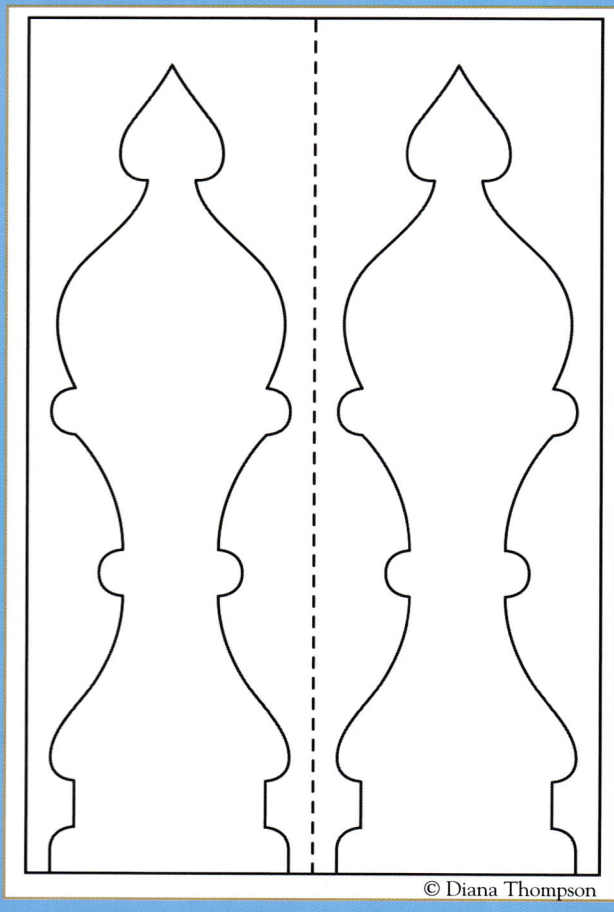

© Diana Thompson

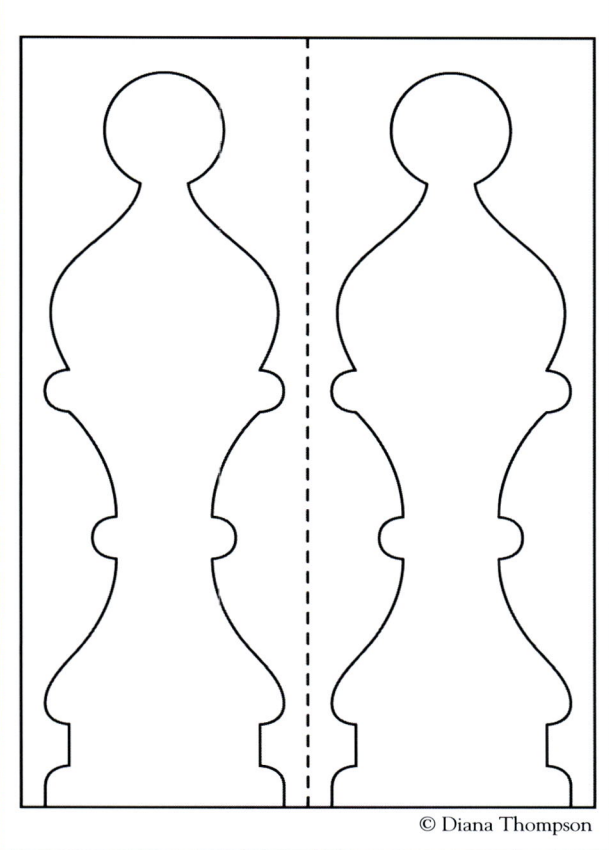

© Diana Thompson

Classic II: Bishop

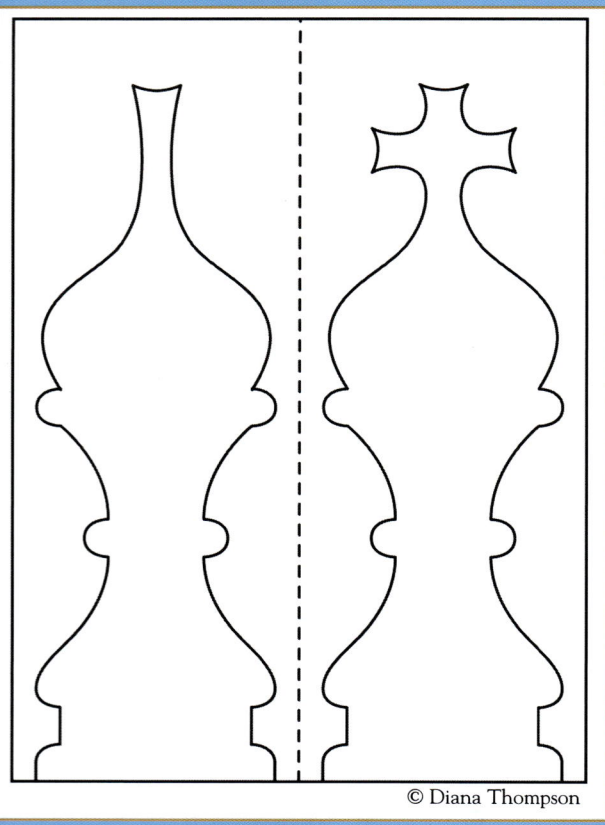

© Diana Thompson

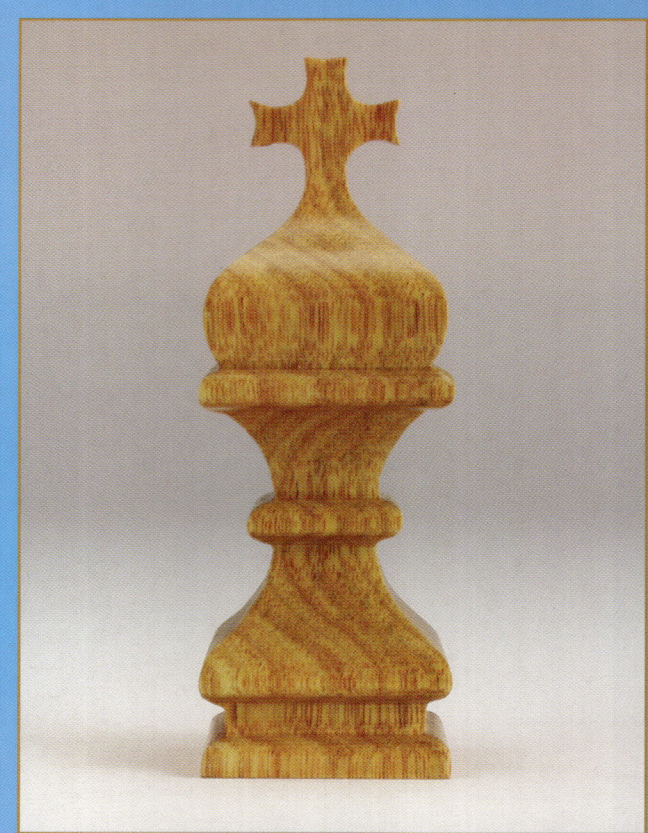

Classic II: Knight

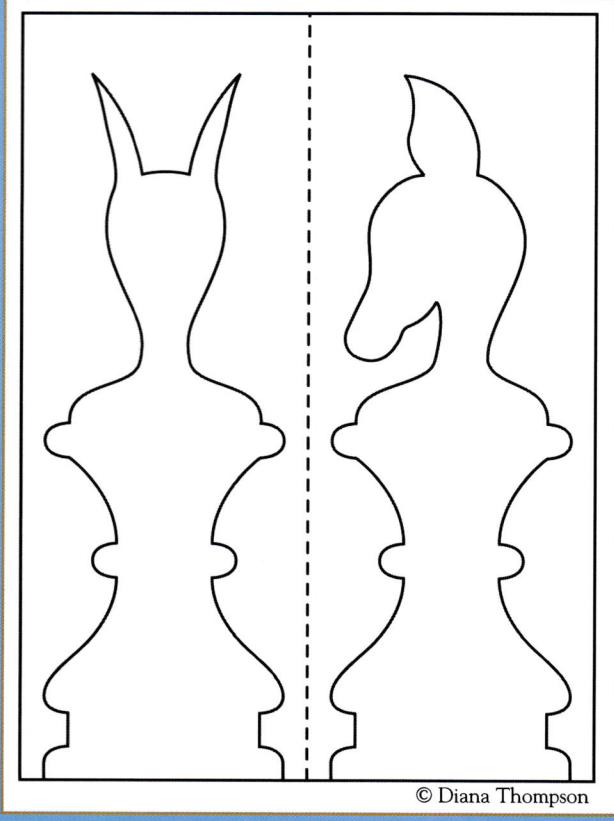

© Diana Thompson

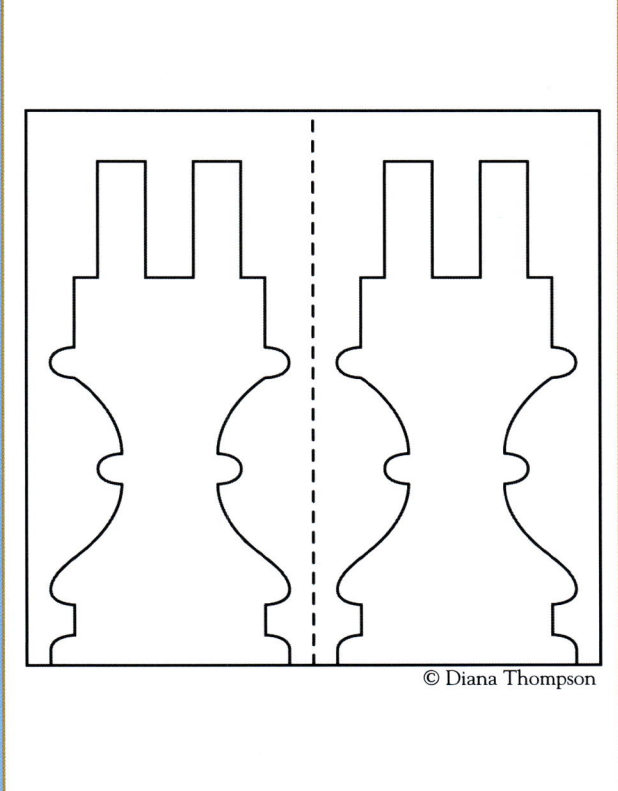

© Diana Thompson

assic II: Pawn

© Diana Thompson

For the Birds

Birds are some of my favorite creatures. I used what I knew about the character of each of these birds to place them in their appropriate places on the chess board. The king is an ostrich, the largest bird. The queen is represented by a flamingo, a beautiful brightly colored bird. The remaining birds all fall into the lesser places on the board with the quail representing the pawn.

Cut each set from a different kind of wood to make each distinctive. This set is cut from Western cedar.

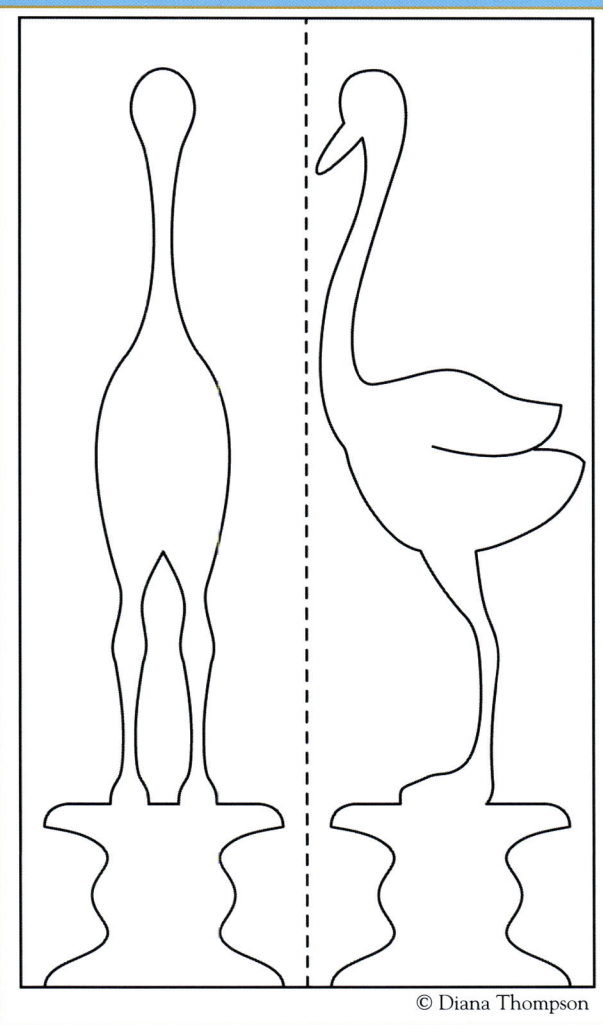

© Diana Thompson

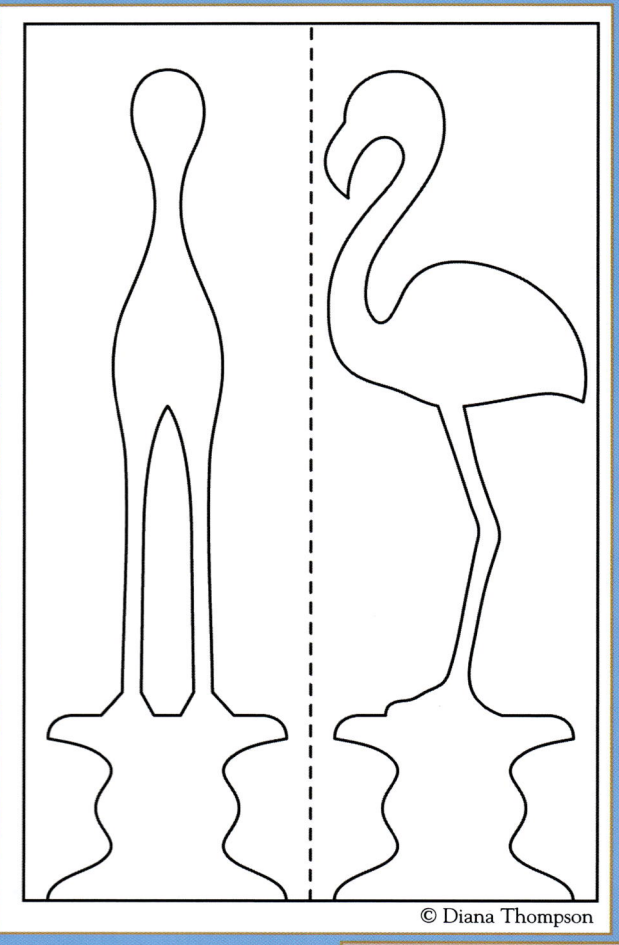

© Diana Thompson

r the Birds: Bishop

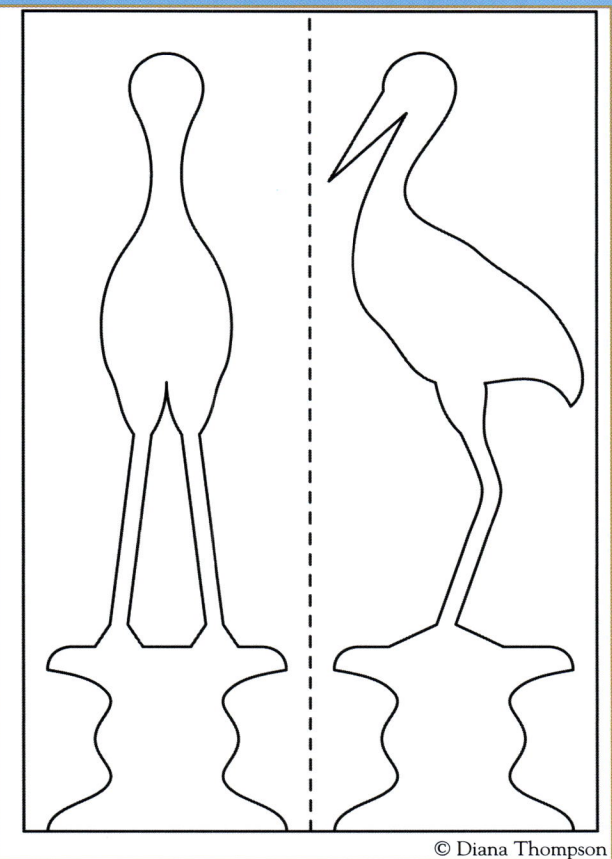

© Diana Thompson

r the Birds: Knight

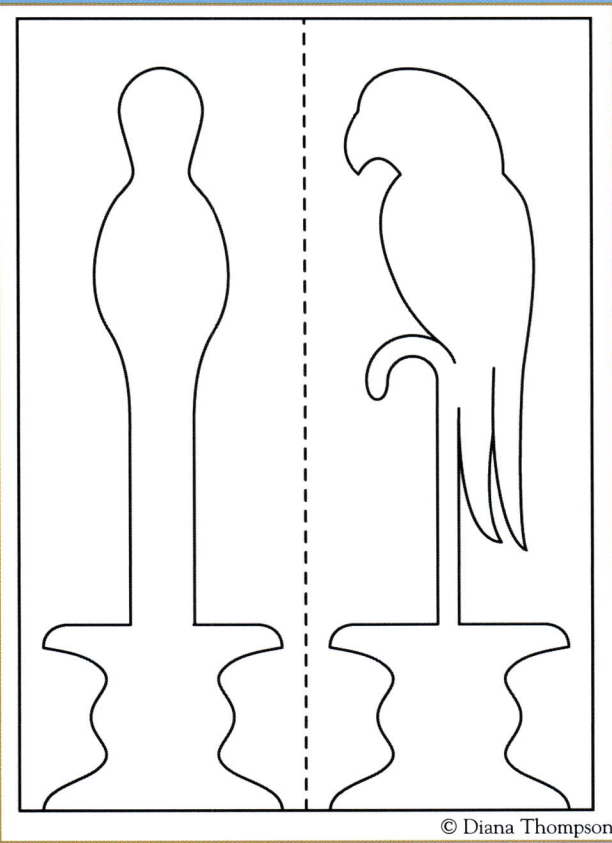

© Diana Thompson

For the Birds: Rook

© Diana Thompson

For the Birds: Pawn

© Diana Thompson

Happy Bugs

Bugs seemed to be naturals for the chess board. The dragonfly became the king, and the butterfly became the queen. Other bugs of nondescript natures filled in the rest of the places on the chess board. Their diminishing sizes gives a clue as to which fills what spot in the game.

Cut each set from a different kind of wood to make each distinctive. This set is cut from red cedar.

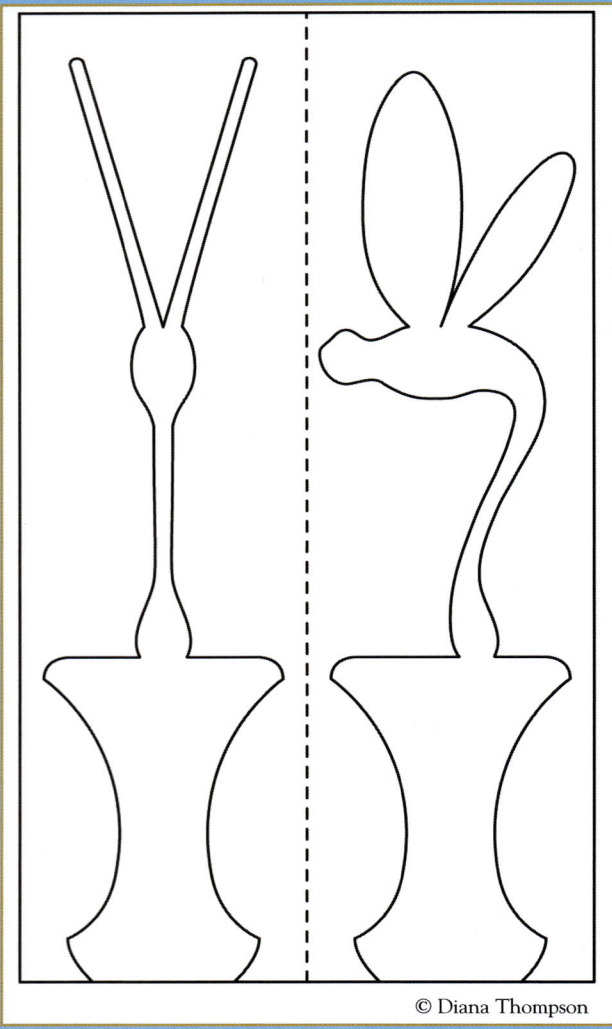

© Diana Thompson

© Diana Thompson

Happy Bugs: Bishop

© Diana Thompson

Happy Bugs: Knight

© Diana Thompson

appy Bugs: Rook

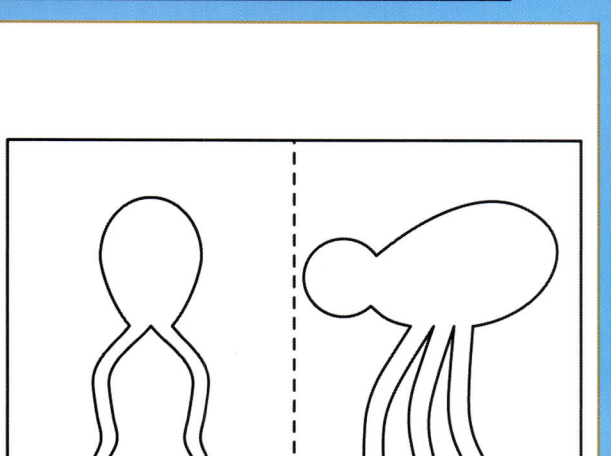

© Diana Thompson

appy Bugs: Pawn

© Diana Thompson

In the Garden

I love to paint, and when the idea came to mind for a garden set, I couldn't let it go. This was a chance to design brightly colored pieces. The tree is the king, and a tulip became the queen. A frog made the perfect bishop, and a shovel became the knight. The rook, following in the tradition of housing, became a bird house. The smallest piece on the board, the pawn, is represented by a growing flower.

Use like colored paints to differentiate the sets. This set is painted with acrylic craft paints.

© Diana Thompson

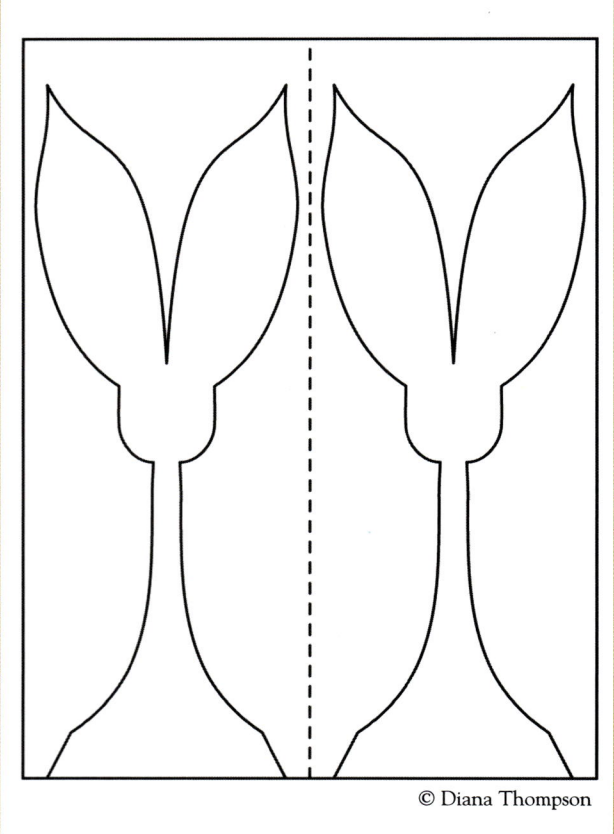

© Diana Thompson

© Diana Thompson

the Garden: Knight

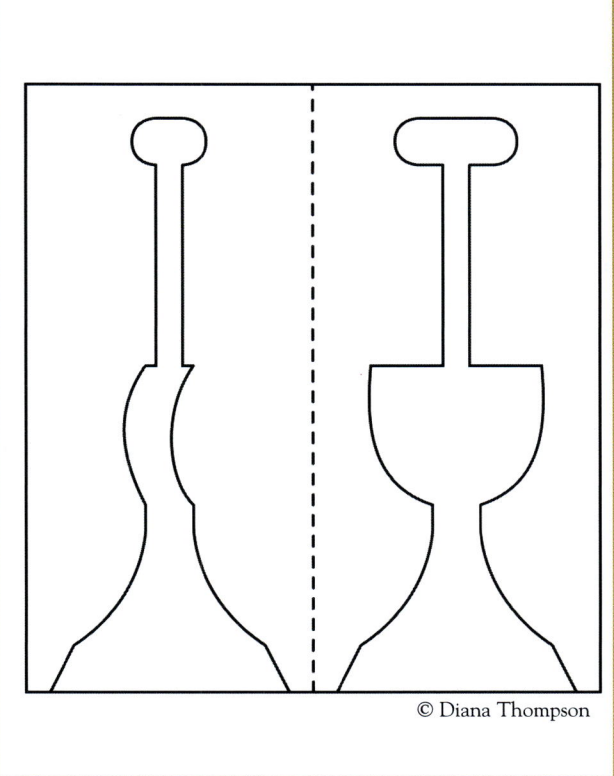

© Diana Thompson

In the Garden: Rook

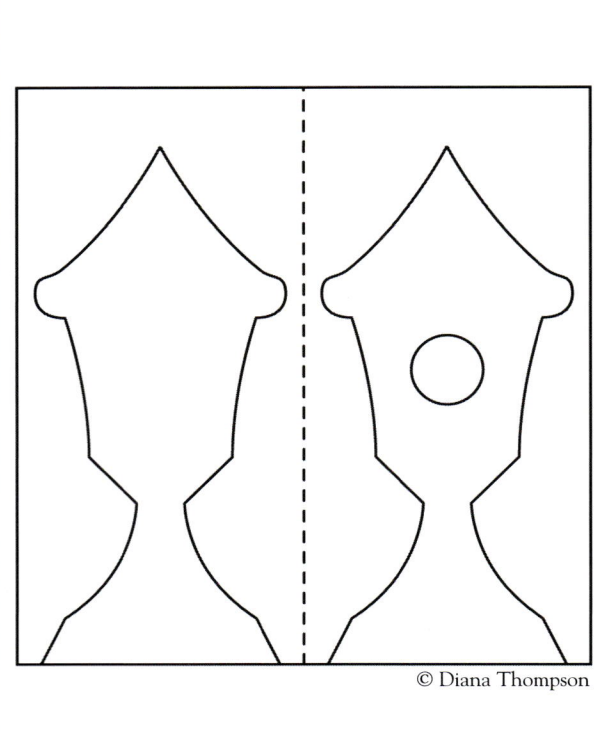

© Diana Thompson

In the Garden: Pawn

© Diana Thompson

Sea Life

The creatures of the deep were another natural for a chess set. Here the shark becomes the king and a tropical fish becomes the queen. The bishop is a rendition of an octopus. The seahorse, while not related to the horse by anything other than name, makes the perfect fit for the knight. Coral, again keeping in the tradition of housing, represents the rook. A seashell makes the perfect pawn.

Cut each set from a different kind of wood to make each distinctive. This set is cut from Makore, also known as African cherry.

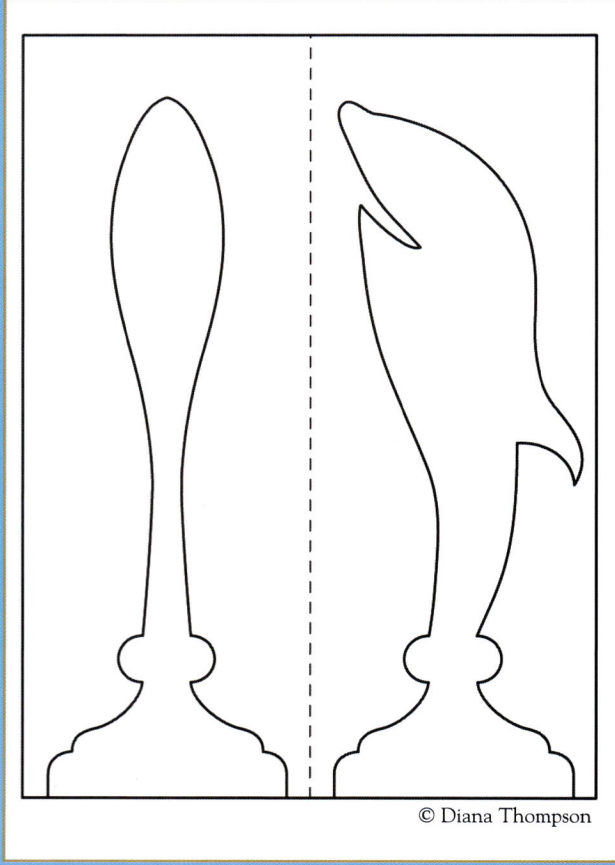

© Diana Thompson

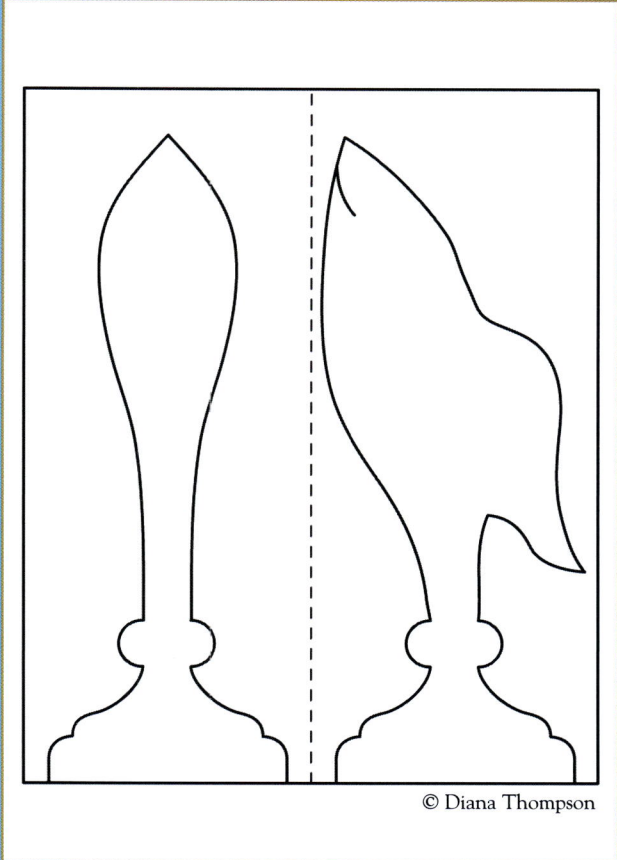

© Diana Thompson

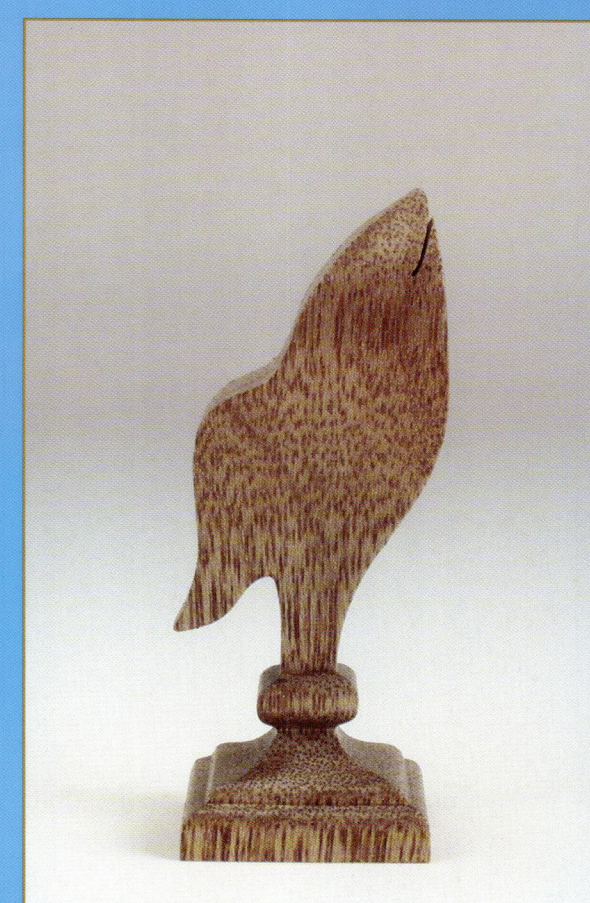

Sea Life: Bishop

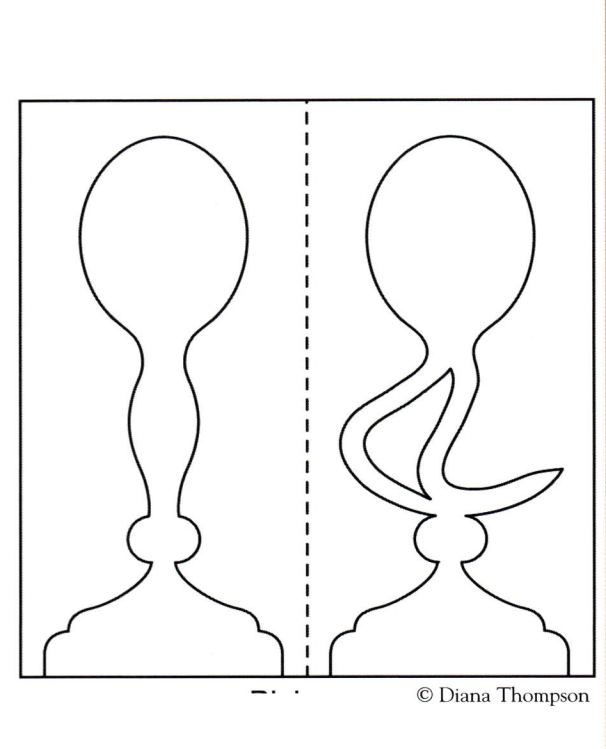

© Diana Thompson

Sea Life: Knight

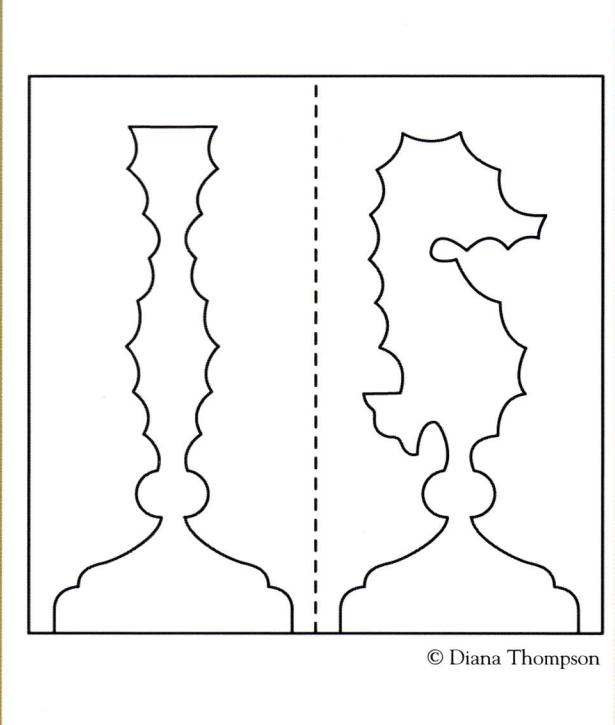

© Diana Thompson

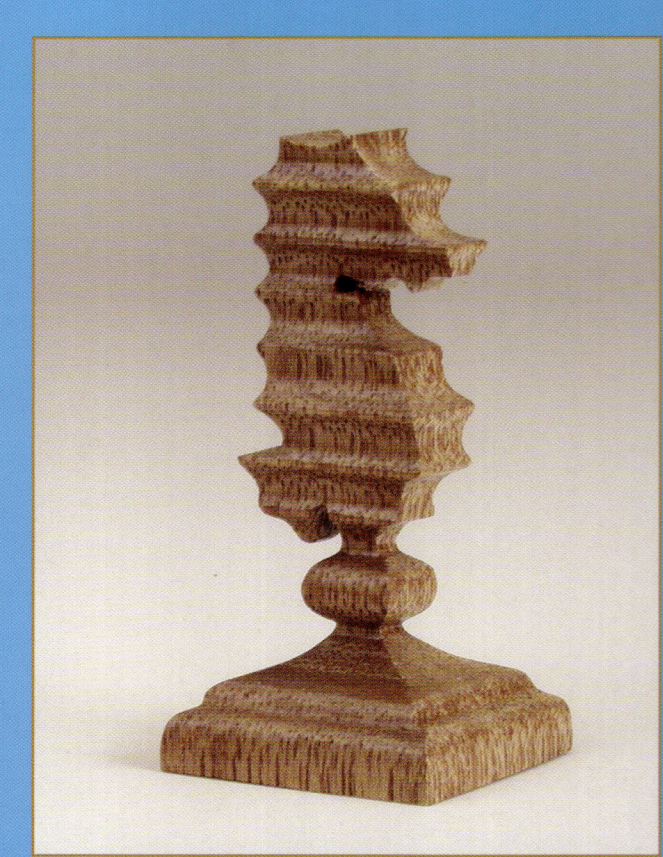

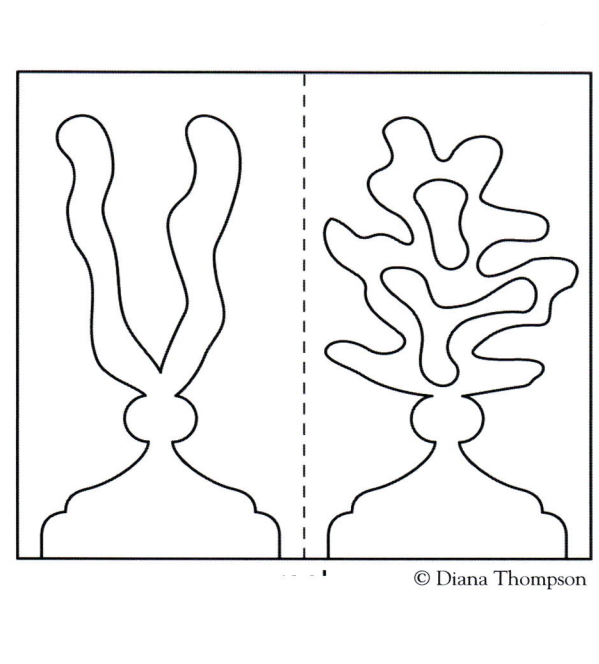

© Diana Thompson

ea Life: Pawn

© Diana Thompson

Alien Chess

While I'm not really a science fiction buff, I know several people who are. This chess set is designed based on my impression of what aliens would look like on a chess board. Each figure follows the same basic pattern. The difference between the figures is found in the wooden balls (available for purchase at many craft and scrolling stores) that are balanced on their tops and the height of the figures themselves. You'll need 1"-diameter balls for the king and queen, ¾"-diameter balls for the bishop and knight, and ½"-diameter balls for the rook and pawn. I used metallic paint to color the balls and then glued them in place to give the figures an out-of-this-world look.

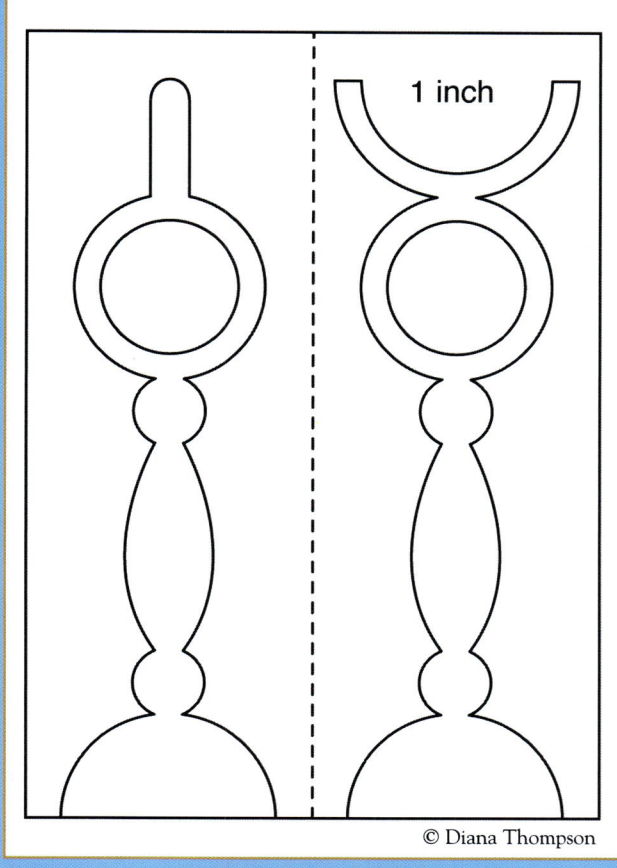

© Diana Thompson

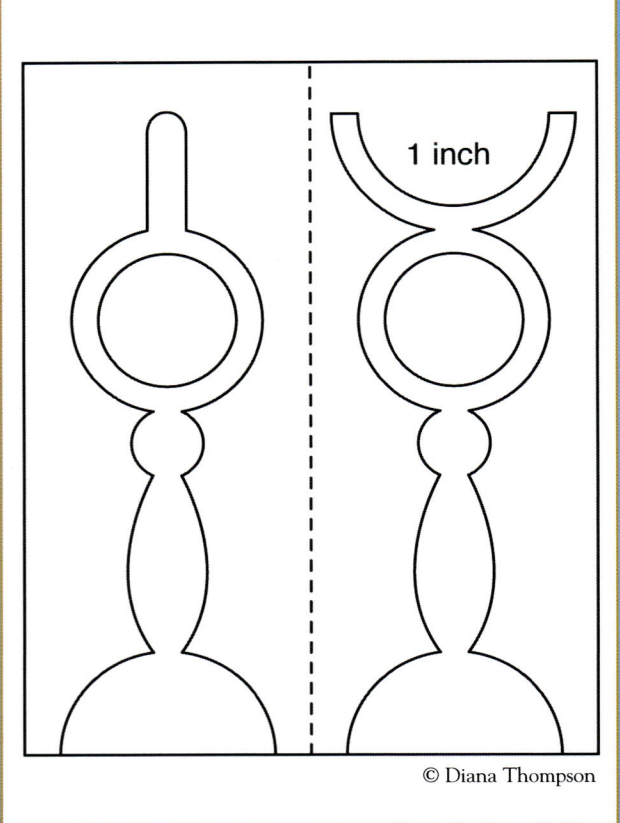

© Diana Thompson

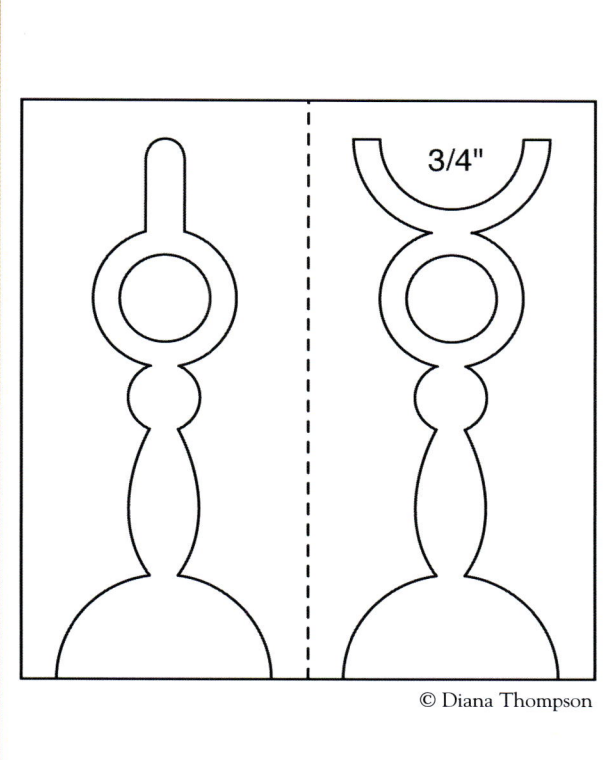

© Diana Thompson

lien Chess: Knight

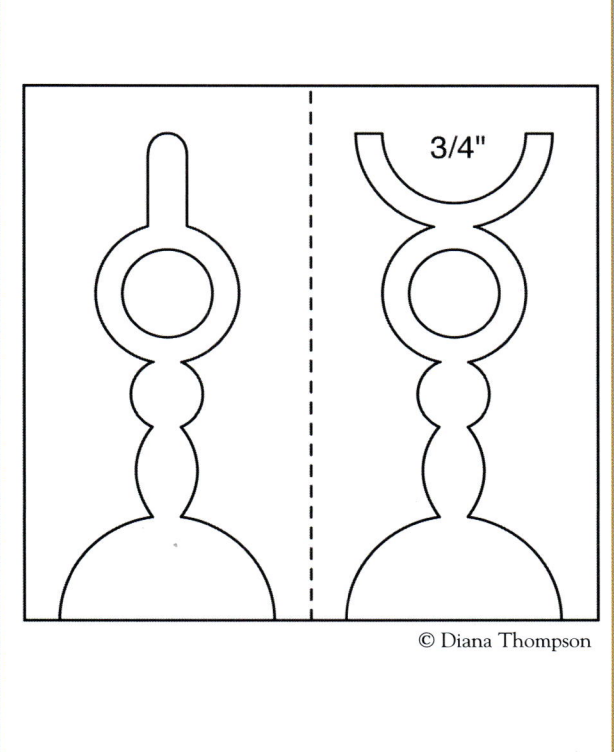

© Diana Thompson

Alien Chess: Rook

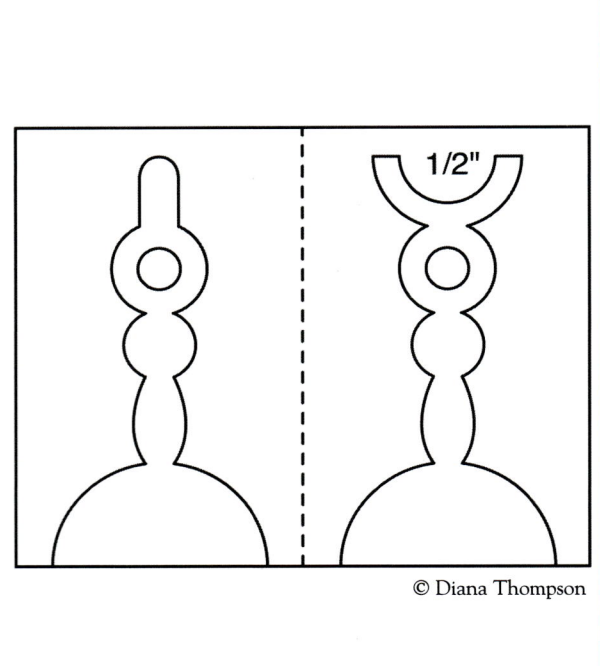

1/2"

© Diana Thompson

Alien Chess: Pawn

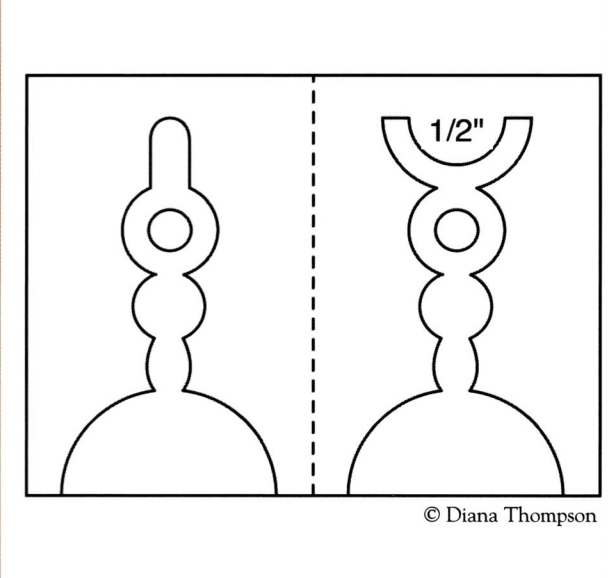

1/2"

© Diana Thompson

Woodworkers Set

Being in my workshop all day designing pieces gave me the idea for this chess set. Each piece is represented by a different tool commonly found in a woodworker's shop. The old-fashioned drill represents the king; a saw, while not overly lady-like, represents the queen. A hammer head, a pliers, a screw driver and a screw represent the remaining pieces on the board.

Cut each set from a different kind of wood to make each distinctive. This set is cut from Spanish cedar.

Woodworkers Set: King

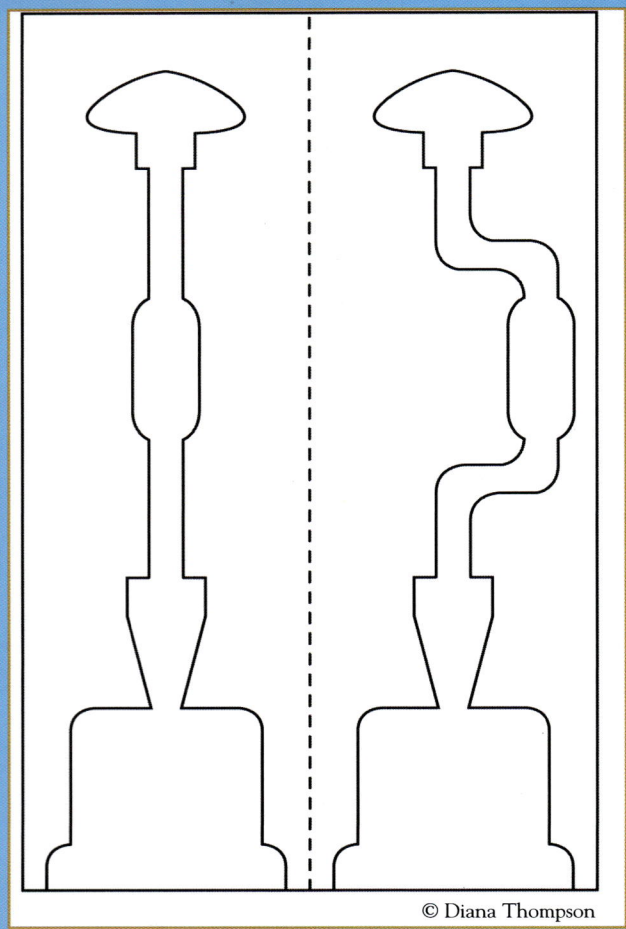

© Diana Thompson

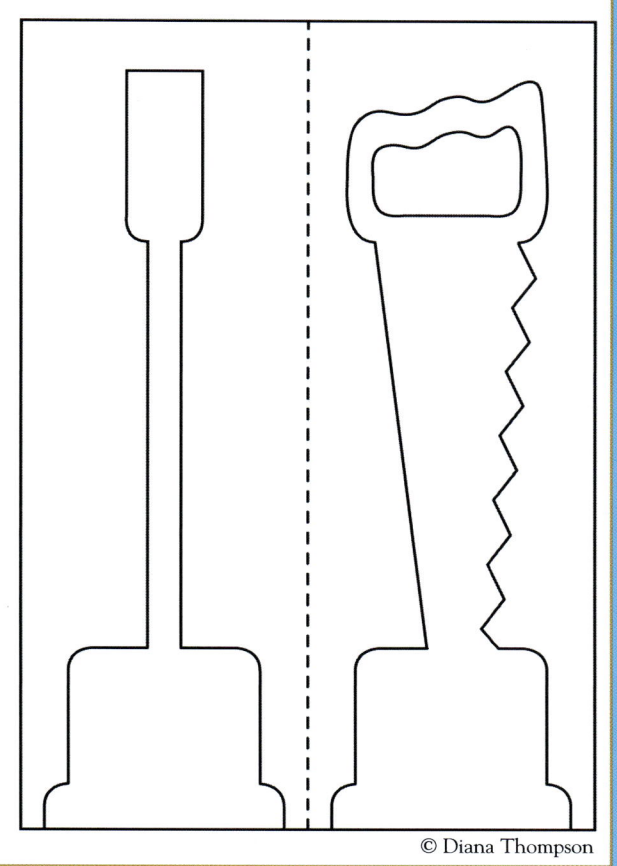

© Diana Thompson

Woodworkers Set: Bishop

© Diana Thompson

Woodworkers Set: Knight

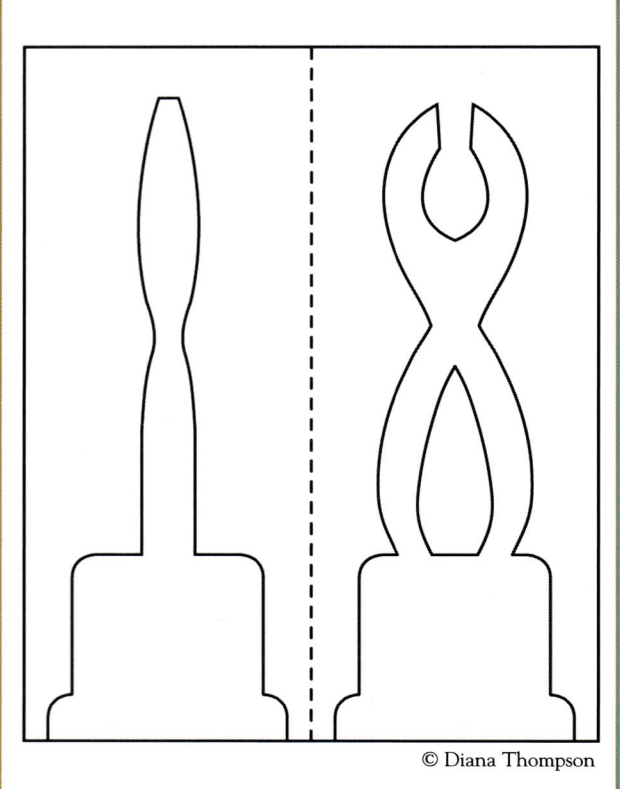

© Diana Thompson

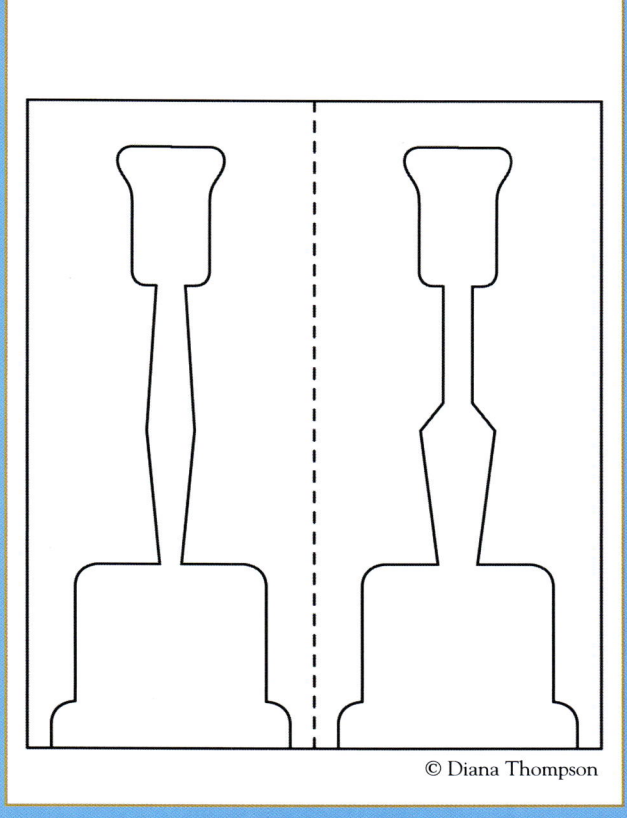

© Diana Thompson

Woodworkers Set: Pawn

© Diana Thompson

Honorable Heritage

I have seen many chess sets that feature different groups of people: soldiers from the Civil War, soldiers from the Revolutionary War, even sports teams. This led me to create a chess set that features Native Americans. A chief with two feathers represents the king, and a princess with one feather represents the queen. Other symbols of Native Americans fill out the rest of the pieces on the board.

This set is cut from willow. Cut each set from a different kind of wood to make each distinctive.

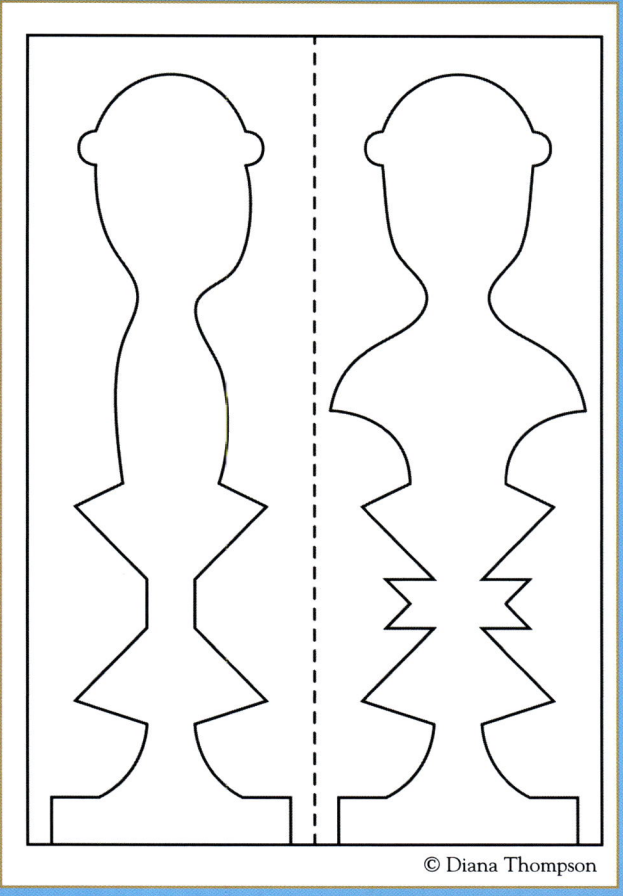

© Diana Thompson

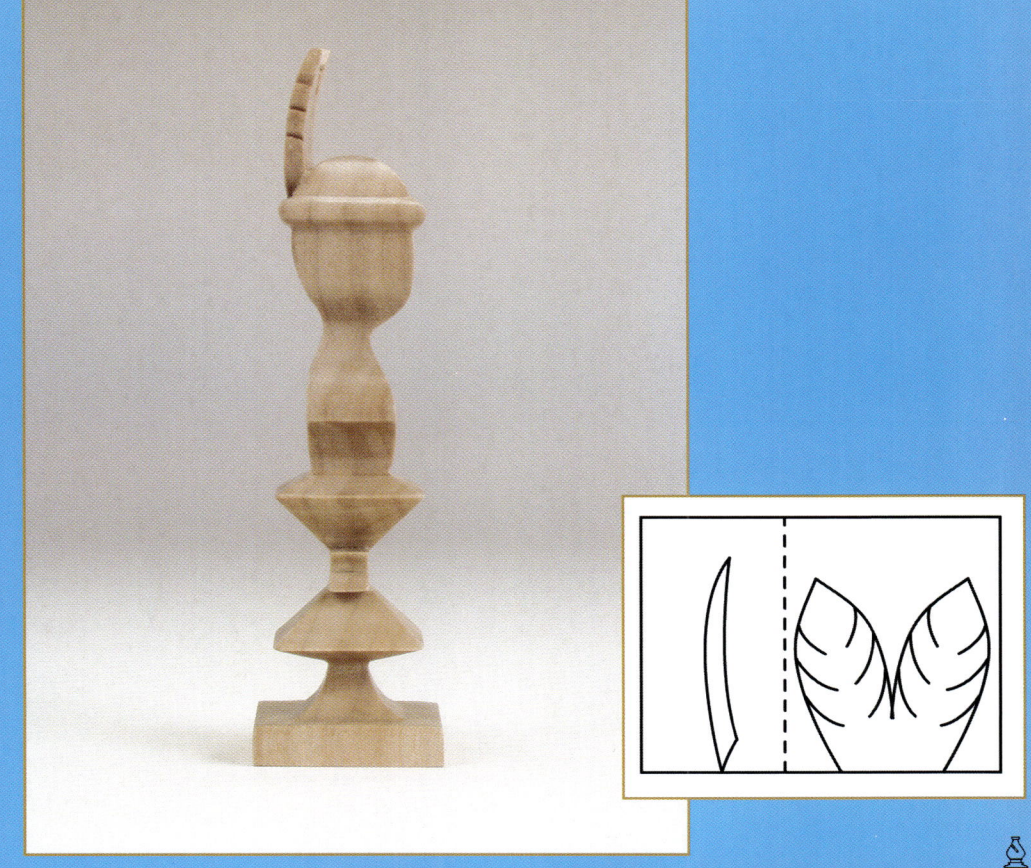

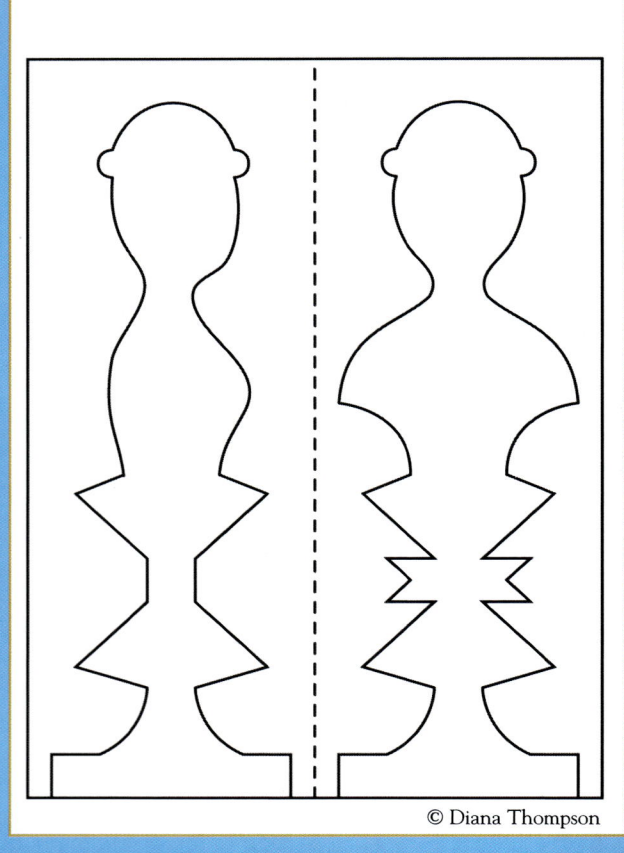

© Diana Thompson

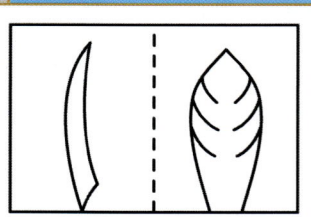

onorable Heritage: Bishop

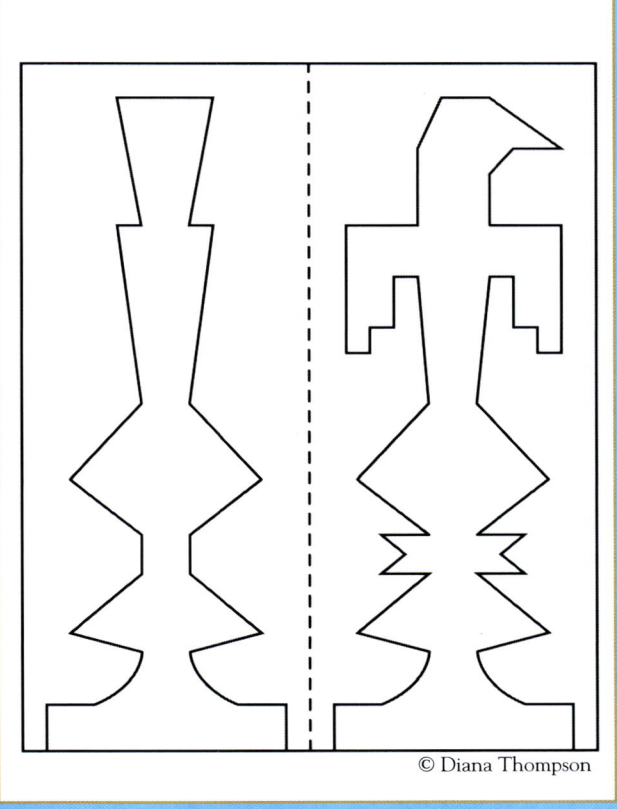

© Diana Thompson

onorable Heritage: Knight

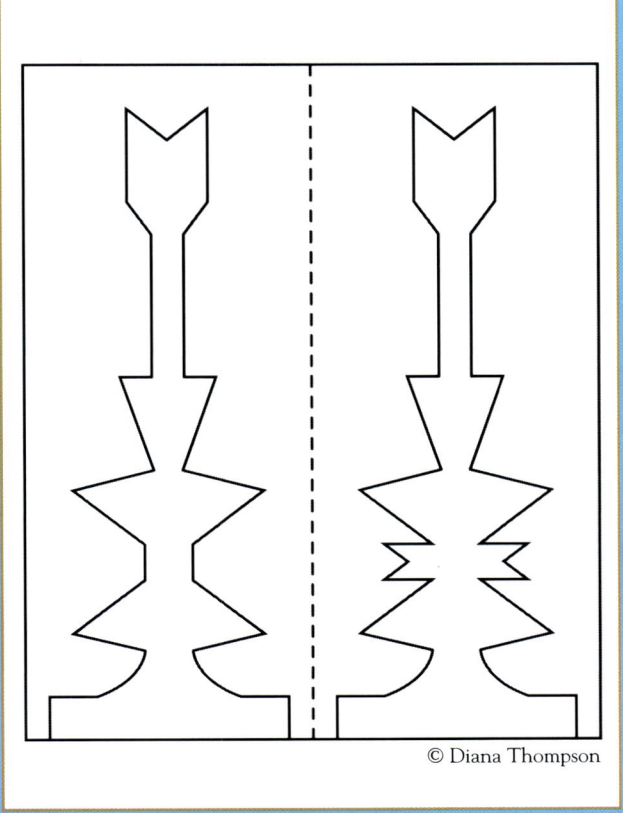

© Diana Thompson

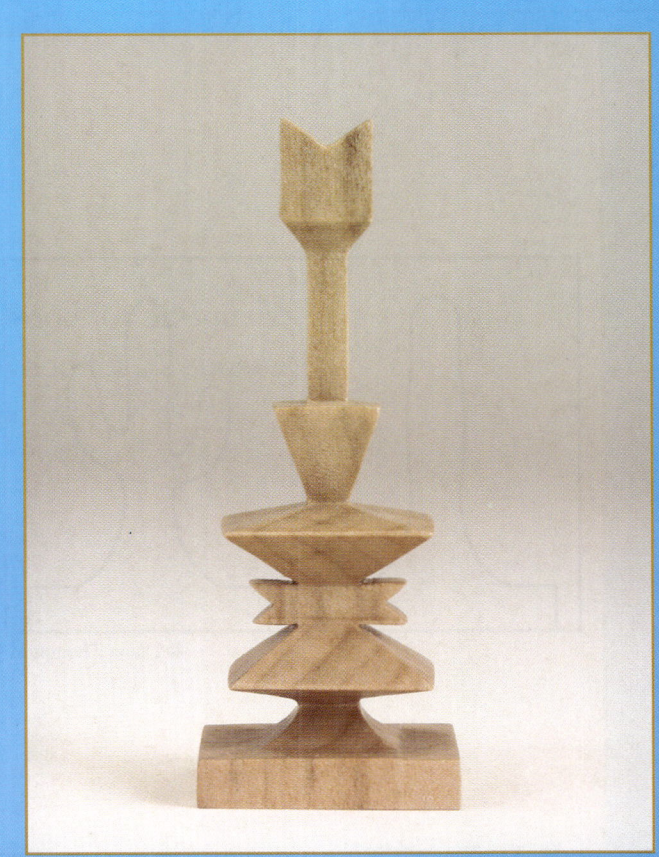

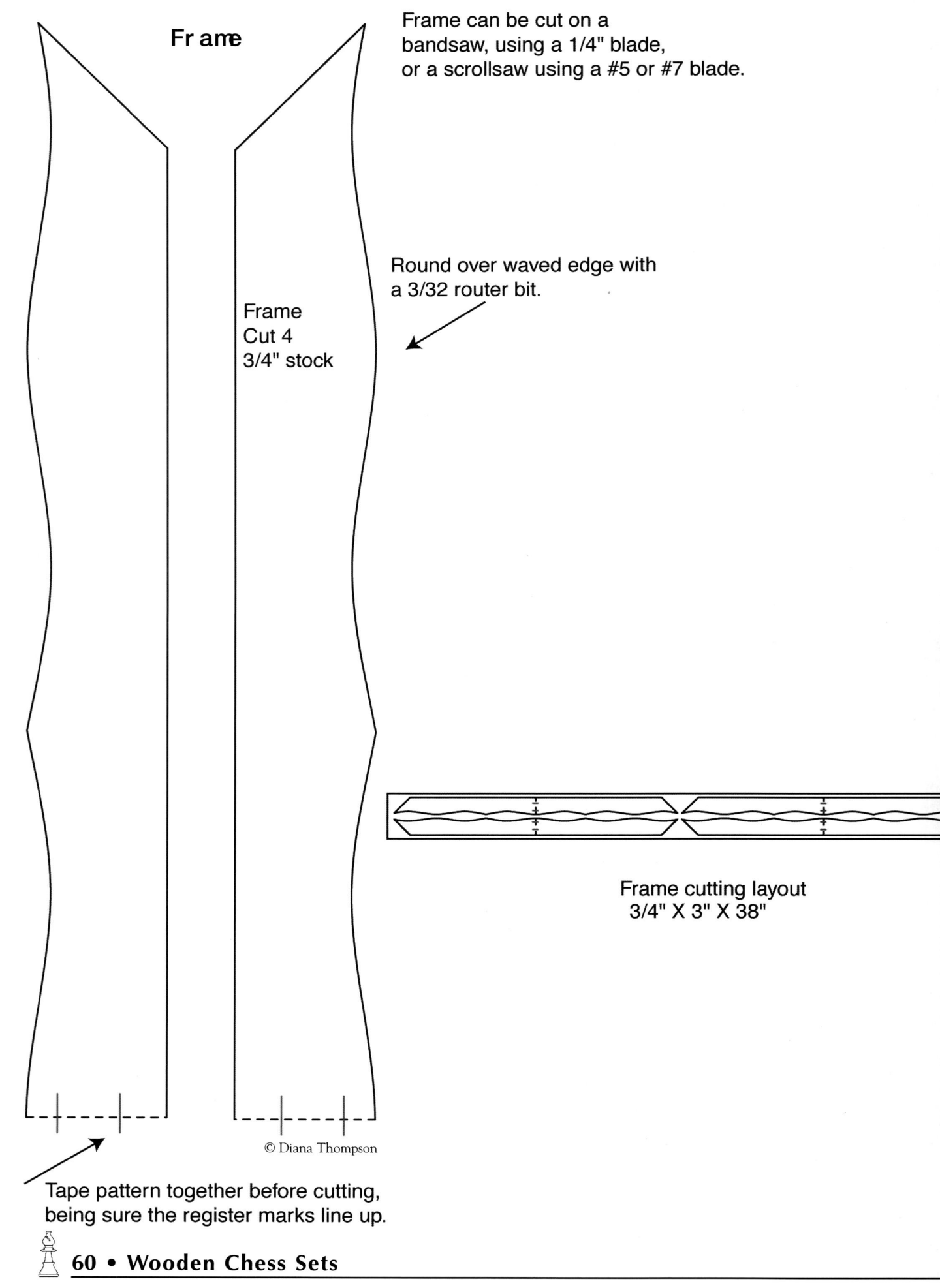

Frame

Frame can be cut on a
bandsaw, using a 1/4" blade,
or a scrollsaw using a #5 or #7 blade.

Frame
Cut 4
3/4" stock

Round over waved edge with
a 3/32 router bit.

Frame cutting layout
3/4" X 3" X 38"

© Diana Thompson

Tape pattern together before cutting,
being sure the register marks line up.

1 Cut slats 2" wide by ¼" thick, making sure that each slat is identical in width and thickness.

2 Square up the slat end with a sander. Do this step before measuring off each consecutive square.

3 Measure and cut a 2" length from the square end of the slat and sand the line away.

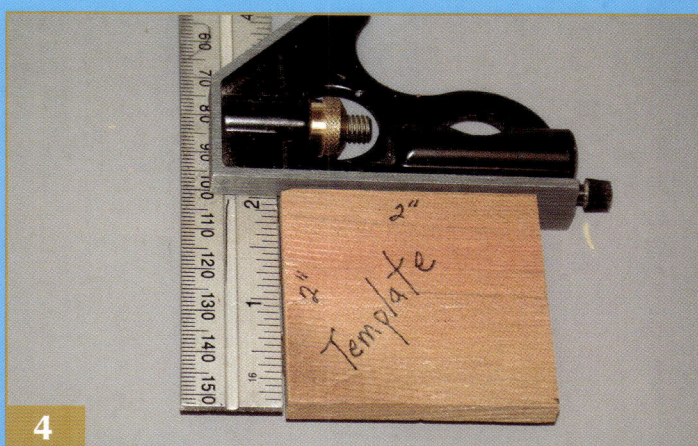

4 Measure the square to make sure it is a perfect 2" square. Label it "template."

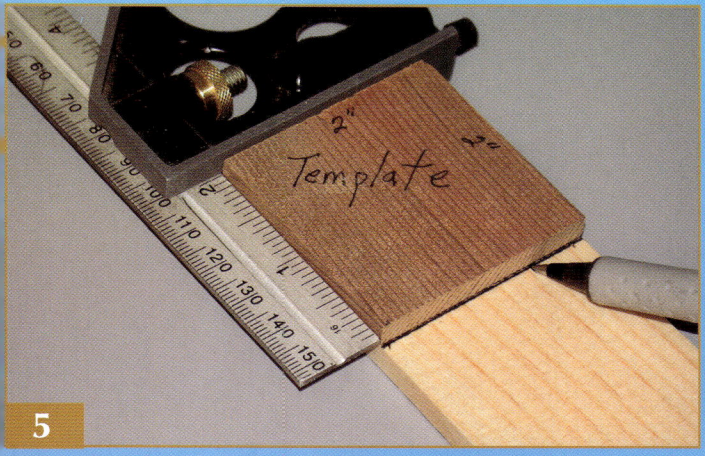

5 Use this template to measure off each square. Measure and cut one square at a time, sanding away the pencil line from each square. Cut 32 light squares and 32 dark squares. Remember to square up the slat end before measuring off the next square.

Gluing the Squares

1 Cut an 18" square of ½" thick plywood for the base. Using a square for alignment, attach two lengths of spare board, 1" wide, to the plywood with screws or nails, leaving a small gap in the corner.

2 This photo shows a close-up of the gap in the corner of the holding area.

3 Place a barrier of waxed paper between the attached boards and the squares. Begin gluing the squares to the plywood, starting in a corner as shown. Apply the glue to the bottom of the squares only, not to the sides.

4 After the glue has set up, remove the alignment boards and trim off the excess plywood.

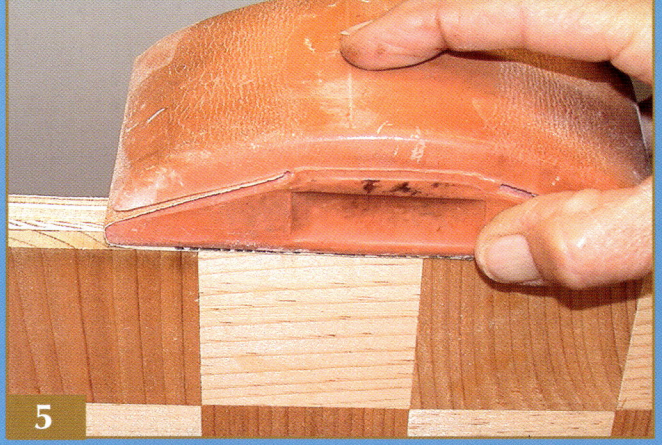

5 Sand the edges smooth with a sanding block.

Making the Frame

1 Cut out the four frame pieces. Sand or cut a 45° angle at each end of each frame piece.

2 Using a 3/32" router bit, rout the top edge of each frame piece.

3 Place a piece of waxed paper on a level surface and glue the corners of the frame together. Use packing tape to hold them until they dry. Before gluing the frame pieces together, do a dry fit to ensure a proper fit.

4 Place the board on a flat surface, with waxed paper underneath. Glue the frame into place.

To finish:
Use a sanding block or an electric hand sander to sand the finished board until it is smooth. Apply a wood sealer. Allow the sealer to dry, then sand the board again. Apply several coats of clear finish and allow the board to dry thoroughly.

Wood for Compound Scrolling

I like to use a wide variety of wood for compound scrolling. The photos in this section will give you a good idea of the different characteristics of many woods. I've based the ease or difficulty of cutting each species on working with 1¹/₂" stock. Any of these woods will cut easily when using thinner stock.

Group I (Very Easy)

1. Sugar Pine
This is the softest and easiest wood to cut. I use it for all my pattern testing and for the figures I plan to paint. This wood is excellent for beginners just learning to compound saw. A very pleasant wood with which to work.

Each sample has been finished with one coat of wood sealer and several coats

2. White Pine
White pine works nearly as well as sugar pine. It also has the advantage of being readily available at most home improvement stores. Look for lumber free of knots and as clear-white as possible. Sometimes it has hard grains that make it a little difficult to cut.

of high-gloss clear acrylic spray.

3. Basswood
This wood is easy to saw and is also a good one to use for painted projects because of its light color. It isn't particularly interesting left in its natural state.

4. Redwood
Redwood is easy to cut. It has a rather dull brown color but finishes nicely. It does have a strong aroma when sawn, but a respirator mask takes care of the odor.

5. Aspen
Aspen has a nice white appearance and a satin sheen when finished. The wood is fuzzy when cut and will dull the blade quickly. This is a good wood for painting because the grain is rather nondescript.

Group II (Easy)

1. Lacewood
This wood has an interesting giraffe-like appearance. Due to the hard and soft areas in the grain, the wood will jump around a little when cutting. Extra effort should be taken to hold the work firmly down on the saw table. Finishes nicely.

5. Heart of the Cypress
A most beautiful, soft golden color and a creamy, velvety appearance are typical of this wood. The heart of cypress does not have the hard grains found in the sapwood. It is a most delightful wood to work with and another of my favorites.

2. Red Cedar
Red cedar has a very beautiful red color and finishes lovely. It also cuts smoothly. The strong aroma calls for a respirator mask. Another of my favorites.

6. Alder
Alder has a nice reddish-brown color. It finishes and cuts fairly easily. Unfortunately, it is not the most interesting of woods as it is usually very uniform in appearance. This sample has a rare appearance.

3. Spanish Cedar
This variety of cedar cuts very easily and finishes nicely. It has a nice golden brown tint, which makes it pleasant in appearance. Very pungent aroma while sawing.

7. Canary Wood
Canary wood has lots of interesting grains and colors, including pink at times. It is easy to cut and finish. I find this wood a pleasure to cut. It is another of my favorites.

4. Willow
This wood is easy to cut and has very interesting grains and colors. It takes a little extra effort to get a smooth finish, but the difficulty is well worth the effort. Another favorite.

8. Ordinary 3/4"
Birch plywood
This wood cuts nicely and has an interesting appearance due to the layers in the product. As with the particle board, glue is used in the manufacturing and will dull the blade quickly.

Group III (Not So Easy)

1. Cypress, sapwood
The sapwood of a cypress tree is a little more difficult to cut than the heartwood, but the prominent grains make it interesting to cut. It reminds me of a zebra. Finishes fairly easily.

2. Mahogany
This wood cuts smoothly and finishes to a beautiful dark, rich color.

3. Magnolia
Magnolia is a most beautiful wood, especially the heart wood. The sapwood is creamy white, but the heartwood has lovely gray to black to purple streaks that make it very interesting. It has a velvety appearance and finishes fantastically! One of my very favorites.

4. Particle board
I tried this material on a whim. It's an interesting concept, and the appearance is different. The only major drawback is the glue used to make the product. It dulls the saw blade quickly.

Group IV (Not Easy At All)

1. Black Walnut
This wood is a woodworkers dream. It cuts smoothly, with little or no sanding, and finishes perfectly. When using it for a bigger figure, you may have to change your blade for the second cut. Be patient and let the saw blade do its work at its own speed. My all-time favorite hardwood.

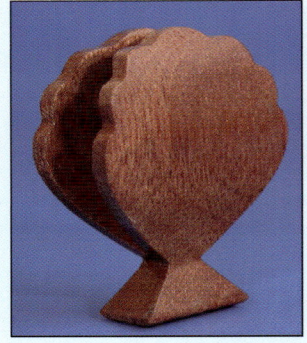

2. Lauan
Lauan is very dense, but it can be used. This wood cuts much like black walnut and finishes fairly nice.

3. Red Oak
I've added this wood because it seems to be a favorite of woodworkers. It cuts similarly to lauan, but it will jump around a bit. Extra effort will be needed to hold the work flat to the saw table. Not my most favorite to use, but it will finish nicely.

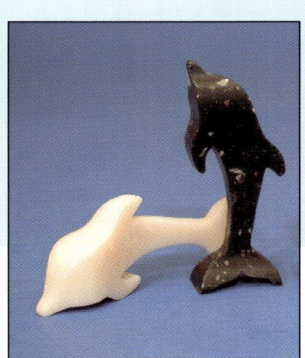

4. Corian®
Corian is a solid surface material, manufactured by Du Pont. It is used mainly for kitchen and bathroom counter tops. Slow the saw speed down to about 1100 strokes per minute, and cover the Corian with masking tape before cutting. These steps will keep the material from melting back onto itself. If you don't see material coming from inside the kerf as you cut, the saw speed is probably too fast. There are several saw blades on the market recommended for cutting solid surface material.

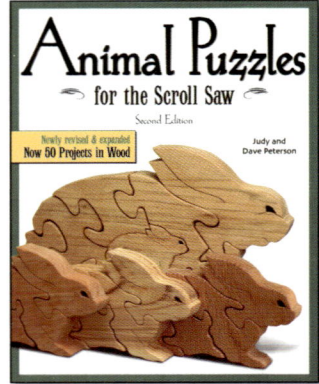
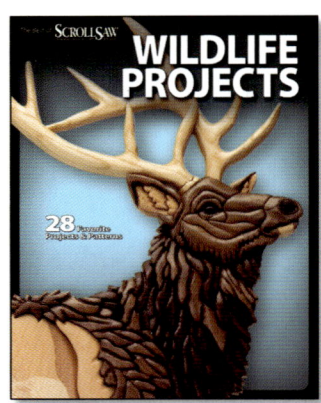
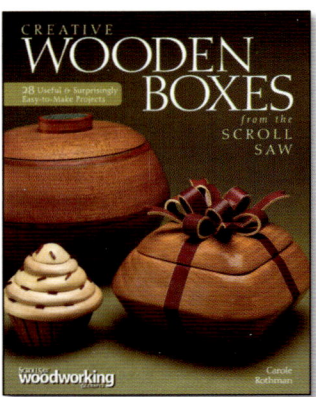